ADVENTURES IN THE FRENCH TRADE

Cultural Memory
in
the
Present

Mieke Bal and Hent de Vries, Editors

ADVENTURES IN THE FRENCH TRADE

Fragments Toward a Life

Jeffrey Mehlman

STANFORD UNIVERSITY PRESS

STANFORD, CALIFORNIA

Stanford University Press
Stanford, California

Printed in the United States of America on acid-free, archival-quality paper

Library of Congress Cataloging-in-Publication Data

Mehlman, Jeffrey.
  Adventures in the French trade : fragments toward a life / Jeffrey Mehlman.
    p. cm. — (Cultural memory in the present)
  Includes bibliographical references.
  ISBN 978-0-8047-6961-7 (cloth : alk. paper) — ISBN 978-0-8047-6962-4 (pbk. :
alk. paper)
  1. Mehlman, Jeffrey. 2. French studies specialists—United States—Biography.
3. Critics—United States—Biography. 4. Litterateurs—United States—Biography.
I. Title. II. Series: Cultural memory in the present.
  DC36.98.M44A3 2010
  944.0072'02—dc22
  [B]

                              2009053332

Typeset by Bruce Lundquist in 11/13.5 Adobe Garamond

For Alicia

And as he saw from the blank faces of the company that nobody understood a word, he answered her as freely as she asked him, speaking, as she did, in perfect French. Thus began an intimacy between the two which soon became the scandal of the Court.
—VIRGINIA WOOLF, *Orlando*

Contents

x   *Contents*

STUDENTS

SEMBLABLES ET FRÈRES

Preface

Walser, by the sheer force of dissociation, and certainly without laying claim to any sort of revelation, patiently slackened all the threads that might have given dignity or consistency to his ego.
—Roberto Calasso, *The Forty-nine Steps*

He seemed constrained by his humor like a madman by his straitjacket.
—Robert Walser, "Mehlmann: A Fairy Tale"

This book is less a chronicle of my life as a scholar/critic of matters French than a series of differently angled fragments, episodes, each with its attendant surprise, in what one commentator has called my *amour vache*, my injured and occasionally injurious love, for France and the French. As such, the reminiscences, readings, letters, and, in one case, fiction that comprise *Adventures in the French Trade* have something of the coherence of a memoir, a protracted speculation on the question of who, more or less (*less* more than *more?*), I will have been.

My reasons for undertaking the project are several. Perhaps foremost is my sense that I have by now been writing long enough to be able to arrive at the kind of insights concerning my own work that I have, up until now, attempted to derive from the reading of others. The discoveries in this realm have for me been bountiful, stunning, and occasionally humbling. They have issued in what is perhaps the centerpiece of this volume, the chapter titled "Chiasmus." A second reason is the fact that for a number of years, and most strikingly in the 1970s, I enjoyed a privileged perch from which to view and be part of the arrival in America of what may be the last of the French vanguards. For about a hundred years, for a large number of people in the West, serious intellectual endeavor has been a matter of thinking with (or against) the French. Think of American poetry without symbolism, American painting without surrealism, a whole strain of American fiction without existentialism, and American academia without deconstruction, and you will understand my point. My presence in New Haven, Ithaca, Berkeley, and Baltimore, French thought's principal ports of call during the 1970s, has supplied me with a host of reminiscences on which I have dined out over the years and which will, I suspect, be of interest to the reader. In addition, my years in Boston have supplied me with the distance from which to gain perspective on the waning of the last of the French vanguards as it has settled into academic respectability. (They have also allowed me to know some remarkably impressive adversaries of the cause to which I have devoted a decade or two of my life.) What I have attempted here is a delineation of how the occasionally polemical episodes I have observed or been embroiled in mesh—and intersect—with textual analyses that have never ceased providing me with exhilaration.

The question of who I will have been is further complicated by the fact that, over the years, there have been enough people who have written, in anger or enthusiasm, as to who, as a critic, I am for me to want to try my own hand, at least in so far as it concerns my life as a reader and writer, at such a delineation. The identifications I have received from others make for a rather intriguing gallery. Early on, in the pages of *Encounter* (the distinguished journal which was also a CIA front), Lionel Abel, who knew André Breton personally, greeted my first book (on autobiography, as it happens) by claiming that in my contentiousness I resembled no one so much as Breton himself, a man who would grab you by the lapels and start shaking you if you so much as suggested that you could bear to look at a Fragonard. Not that many years later, my book on legacies of anti-Semitism in France had a reviewer in the *Nouvelle revue française* claiming that my true affinity was with Stavrogin, one of Dostoyevsky's *Possessed.* (On that occasion I learned the meaning of the much-abused word "collegiality" when a Slavist in my department told me not to worry: if you had to be one of the "possessed," Stavrogin was definitely the one you would want to be.) On the other side of the ledger, more recently, in the *TLS,* George Steiner, with consummate generosity, proposed (*toute proportion gardée*) that I was in fact, in what he called my "scholastic wit," rather similar to Walter Benjamin. And finally Régis Debray, no less generously, in a finely wrought piece, opined that I was doing—or perhaps better, trying to do—for French literary history what Robert Paxton had done for French political history.

Imagine then a room, or better, an ongoing card game, bridge, gathering these four alter egos: Breton and Stavrogin, the possessed, would surely be partnered (as Drieu la Rochelle more or less saw in his novel *Gilles*), and they'd be playing against the tandem formed by Benjamin and Paxton. And the game itself, from this perspective, would, at some level, be, well . . . *me*.

The conceit of the allegedly sovereign subject as a card game has its charms. Queneau, after all, took pleasure in writing the name Descartes in two words, as *des cartes* (even as Mallarmé, who will wend his way through these pages, was of the thought that thought itself, ultimately, was reducible to a crap shoot). In the coda to this book the reader will encounter a more far-reaching interlingual pun on the name of France's premier philosopher. In the meantime, those four adversaries at bridge will have served to introduce the reader to several of what some have identified as the principal players in my mind.

About twenty years ago, I made my sole appearance, to my knowledge, in a novel. That circumstance is not unrelated to the existence of this book. In *My Strange Quest for Mensonge*, the British novelist and sometime judge of the Booker Prize, Malcolm Bradbury, delivered himself in 1988 of an academic fiction concerning the effort to write a biography of a deconstructionist academic who had pressed his craft to such an extreme that he had quite simply self-deconstructed—or vanished. A bit heavy-handed, to be sure, but not without its lessons. In his search for the eponymous Mensonge, the protagonist, in his frustration, makes his way through the indexes of every available guide to contemporary criticism, all to no avail: the indexes invariably go directly from "Mehlman, Jeffrey" to "Merleau-Ponty, Maurice" with nary a trace of the evanescent Henri Mensonge. No more than a cameo appearance, to be sure (my most memorable moment coming in the novel's fictive index, where my name is followed by the clarification: "his role in indexes"), but one that has remained with me over the years. As decades have passed and I find myself a bit less frequently listed in the indexes of critical guides, I am inclined, before I too go the way of Henri Mensonge, to offer a corrective to Bradbury's preposterous conceit and show just how indelible a mark the deconstructive sensibility can leave in one's sense of self.[1]

The ultimate deconstruction, of course, is of the flesh and awaits us all. I pen this preface, the book now complete, while waiting to undergo the "green light laser" of what is billed as a minor operation tomorrow. The light-cutting edge to the extent that it requires no cutting—will vaporize, I'm told, the excess tissue of an organ that had become so much the area of expertise of the physician brother of a famous novelist that it was long referred to in certain French circles as the "proustate."

All benign, but a first intimation of mortality . . . It was Paul Valéry, who in a poem called "Le Vin perdu," once found himself haunted by the image of a senseless pouring of "just a bit" of red wine into water, then watching it dissolve in a "pink mist," never to return. The image, it turned out, was originally used by the physicist Poincaré to illustrate entropy, the irreversibility of time: the red drops of wine could never be retrieved. Valéry incorporated the image into his poem, but also into his classic essay, "Crise de l'esprit," where it served as the vehicle of his distress upon realizing that the "improbable" treasure of European intelligence was beginning to trickle out into an impoverished world from which it could never be recovered. The poet was upset. But can any male of my age doubt that the telltale image of drops of wine poured into water and the ensuing distress capture transparently the shock of finding blood in one's urine? Small wonder, then, that the poet should attempt to resolve the enigma, dispel the image, which obsessed him, by turning himself into a Eurologist . . .

What follows is a story that begins with an anecdote—or fantasy—relating to blood. It is perhaps fitting that I should conclude this preface with words written on—if not quite in—that very same fluid.

The operation is tomorrow at noon.

DECEMBER 19, 2***

ADVENTURES IN THE FRENCH TRADE

1

Beginning and End

One grows up with the stoical passions of a would-be hero and ends up, with any luck, an epicurean, savoring pleasures too nuanced and fleeting to be compatible with the monumental aspirations of youth. The template is from Montaigne but carries a validity that stretches at least as late as the *Antimémoires* of Malraux: an all too Western world of Resistance heroics yields to an aesthetic realm of ongoing metamorphosis as the author-psychonaut makes his way to India and points east. I too appear to have followed the template, but in my own case what strikes me is how *French* the fantasies informing beginning and end, the stoical and the epicurean, turn out to have been.

The beginning: It all made sense, the kind of fantastical sense that has always intrigued me, when I one day attended to the specifics of one of the family legends of my youth. I had been, I was told, a miracle child, not by virtue of any talents but by dint of my survival. I had been born in 1944 with a hematological complication resulting from what was beginning to be known as RH factor, a condition that at the time was tantamount to a death sentence for the newborn child. The miracle was that I was one of the first children in medical history (or at least in the medical history of Yorkville, the New York City neighborhood in which I was born) to avert the curse through a total blood transfusion. No doubt the sense of threat was compounded by the fact of being born a Jew in 1944 in the deeply German neighborhood of Yorkville. But it was only years later that the true allure of my survival, its coherence with a life attending to matters French, was revealed to me. For the RH condition, I learned, was in fact the result of a reaction of rejection induced in the mother by the birth of a previous child. Now, it happens that my mother, who knew not a word of French, was named Frances. And my elder brother just happened to be born on June 13, 1940, the day of the entry of the Nazis into Paris. Under the circumstances could I have any more apt task in life, which I entered in the glory days of the Resistance, than to liberate occupied France(s)? And thus it may have been that the well nigh universal tendency to stoical heroics that affects many a youth should choose, in my case, the world of the anti-Nazi Resistance as its arena.

After the stoical, the epicurean. Some years ago I found myself particularly drawn to a strikingly trivial poem of Mallarmé. It was a mere four lines in length and was addressed—indirectly—to one of the poet's friends, Louis Metman:

Tant de luxe où l'or se moire
 N'égale pas, croyez-m'en,
Vers! dormir en la mémoire
De Monsieur Louis Metman.

Not all that shimmering gold, the poet teases his verse, could equal the sheer luxury of reposing in the recesses of the memory of the poet's esteemed friend. Yes, one wanted to say, there could be no more lavish pleasure than to find oneself the site in which the various intricacies of Mallarmé's poems would emerge from their dormant state and coalesce into new coherence. Indeed, for years Mallarmé had struck me as a limit case in literature, and I had secretly coveted the prospect, as a critic, of disclosing a Mallarméan dimension in writers one would otherwise not suspect of such an affinity. Yet the words *dormir* and *mémoire de-*"sleeping" in "memory of"—pointed to a second dimension that seemed almost funereal; and it was then, upon realizing that this exquisite quatrain was no doubt the only poem in the French language in which I could substitute my own name (at the rhyme, no less!), without any appreciable poetic loss, that I found myself indulging the plagiarist's fantasy of having stumbled upon my own ideal epitaph. Surely, to have spent one's life as the locus in which the implicit intricacies of a great poet's work might achieve their maximal resonance would not be a negligible way of summing up an existence. Not in all the pages of the great Blanchot has the intimate bond between *l'espace littéraire* and death—that "all too shallow stream," a *peu profond ruisseau*, as the poet calls it—affected me as deeply as in my plagiarist's fantasy of an epitaph to die for.

Initiation: Bécheron

The annual holiday party at the R*** home, just off Harvard Square, was always a pleasure, with its assortment of local literary types and ample punch bowl, but this year's celebration was slightly different for us. Our son was arriving that night from college and was now so presentable, so alert, that it seemed almost an act of generosity on our part to ask to bring him with us. There were the affinities, of course. Ezra was completing his studies at Washington University in St. Louis, the university founded by the grandfather of T. S. Eliot, and our host's distinction was such that he had been granted by Eliot's widow the assignment of editing the juvenilia of the St. Louis–born poet. Each, that is, represented differently a legacy of the family Eliot. Then there was the sheer grace of our host. It was more than ten years earlier that Ezra had first caught sight of Christopher R***. He had come to a dinner at our home and immediately walked over to our then six-year-old son and introduced himself: "Hi, my name is Christopher. I'm fifty-nine; how old are you?" Coming in Christopher's Oxbridge English, the introduction had made an impression on Ezra, and I could sense that he was not uninterested in seeing what a decade or more could do to a fifty-nine-year-old.

I had another reason for being happy to bring our son along. My first night in France, forty-five years earlier, happened to have found me, an exhausted sixteen-year-old, arriving near midnight at a comparably elegant (and emphatically European) gathering. The venue was Bécheron, a sixteenth-century manor in Touraine. That evening had a determinative effect on the course of my life. I still dimly recall the elegantly angled cigarette holders, the men in smoking jackets, the appreciative smiles of

a series of stylish French women as they welcomed me (in French I struggled to understand) to what was the fiftieth-birthday party of their host,
the owner of the manor. Forty-five years later, at the holiday gathering
chez R***, attire was informal, there were no cigarette holders (or, for that
matter, cigarettes), but there was a palpable and very *adult* elegance in the
air, and I had the wistful thought that my son, in a position to take it all
in, might know an elation in some way comparable to the one that I had
experienced that late June night in 1960.

Our hostess, Judith A***, was a photographer. She had done a number of portraits of literary eminences, many of whom had no doubt come
her way through her marriage to Christopher. At present, I learned, she
was planning an album of such literary portraits for publication, an attractive proposition which put me in mind of a memoir I had recently been
reading by an American portrait sculptor of the first half of the twentieth
century, Jo Davidson. As we approached the punch bowl, I mentioned that
her current project reminded me of the impressively illustrated volume,
Between Sittings, of a portraitist she might or might not have heard of, one
Jo Davidson. Whereupon her eyes lit up, she expressed a measure of disbelief, and told me that she was very much aware of Jo Davidson's sculp-
ture, since his works were everywhere to be found in the sixteenth-century
manor, Bécheron, in Touraine, where she had spent a number of unforgettable days during a fabulous summer of her early adolescence. I was the
first person she had met in fifty years who had also been there. Whereupon
I had the pleasure of compounding her surprise by telling her that not only
was that not—quite—the case, but that another guest at her party that
evening had had a comparably indelible impression of Bécheron at midcentury. She was the novelist-journalist Renata A***, then engaged in conversation with a graduate student on the other side of the room.

As the three of us gathered to share recollections of the place, it occurred to me that all three of us (and here I take the license, *le punch
aidant*, of conflating host and hostess, Christopher and Judith) had something else in common. All three of us, Christopher, Renata, and myself,
had suffered in one way or another for expecting that others (and, it is
to be hoped, ourselves) live up to extremely—perhaps excessively—high
standards. The most spectacular case was Renata's. A prominent critic in
the pages of the *New Yorker*, the *New York Times*, and the *New York Review
of Books* from a young age, she had recently suffered a fall in public esteem

after publishing a rather vitriolic attack on the most prestigious of the three, which, to the disbelief, then anger, of much of the journalistic elite, she declared to be "dead" in the first sentence of her book. The journalistic closing of ranks in the face of this assault against the most revered of its sacred cows was perhaps to be expected. But it was the *hauteur* of Renata's tone from the beginning which no doubt put her in the sights of those who eventually made her their target. Here is one evocation of that tone that I culled from an online journal: "You never knew, when you began [one of her] reviews, whether you would finish it upset at the sharp cruelty of her tone or elated at her knack for getting what's wrong with a movie exactly right." It was, presumably, the elevation of those standards that accounted for the off-putting cruelty of the tone.

As for Christopher, the eminence of his accomplishments granted him a certain immunity, but within the university his relations with his colleagues in the English Department, none of whom could be other than admiring of his work, had become so vexed that he had seceded from the department, setting up shop in another precinct of the university. It seemed probable to me that that vexation had something to do with holding his colleagues to standards they felt less than comfortable attempting to meet. As for myself, I have mellowed considerably over the years, but I take it that there must have been an element of truth in a review of my first book, in *Encounter*, claiming that my contentiousness of tone, in its intolerance, reminded the reviewer of no one so much as André Breton. Several years ago, the then master of Christ's College, Cambridge, visiting Boston, quipped that when he read my first book, he encountered a tone of such startling "self-assurance" that his initial impulse was to close up shop and change professions. (Happily for the future of criticism he did not.) I have always assumed that when, in 1979, I was denied tenure (shortly after my nemesis, fresh from his much-touted critique of sacrificial violence, informed me that the university in which we both taught was the only one in the country in which I might be denied tenure and that he was going to make sure that happened), one of the reasons that the profession as a whole failed to rush to my rescue was relief, perhaps delight, that so much "self-assurance" should be followed by a fall . . .

Three figures at the holiday party that night—Renata, Christopher (*par épouse interposée*, such cases of conjugal contagion being more common than is appreciated), and myself—had had an indelible exposure to the charms of Bécheron, and all three had suffered for their exaggeratedly high standards. Might there be a connection? It all put one in mind of certain analyses of anti-Semitism. The specialty of Judaism, as George Steiner memorably put it, was a certain "blackmail of the ideal," precisely what I have called exaggeratedly high standards, which led him to conclude: "Of this pressure, I believe, is loathing bred."[1] There was, then, something faintly religious about this communion of souls around a privileged site, Bécheron, and the call to transcendence seeming to issue from it. It is time to speak of that shrine.

*

My story with Bécheron, the sixteenth-century manor in the town of Saché, twenty miles from Tours, begins before my birth, when the property was acquired, in 1927, by the sculptor Jo Davidson, whose name had so surprised Judith A*** at the holiday party just evoked. Davidson, a New Yorker, born in 1883, was adventurous enough to have exhibited in the legendary Armory exhibition of 1913, but was above all a remarkably successful portrait sculptor, whose success, beyond any aesthetic criterion, might be gauged by the number of early-twentieth-century eminences who sat for him. They ranged from Joseph Conrad and James Joyce, Anatole France and André Gide, to John D. Rockefeller and Andrew Mellon, Woodrow Wilson and Franklin Roosevelt—not to mention D. H. Lawrence and Rudyard Kipling, Frank Sinatra and Benito Mussolini. Will Rogers called him "the last of the savage head hunters."[2] He was, in his way, the Richard Avedon of clay. And the fact that his way of working was to come to know his subject by getting him or her to talk (rather than hold still) must have made of him an endless source of irresistible anecdotes, some of which he recorded in the memoir I had mentioned to Judith A***, *Between Sittings*.

He was also a Francophile. The comment I had retained from a reading of his memoir years earlier was by Joseph Conrad. The great Pole, while sitting for the sculptor, insisted on speaking to him in French, a circumstance which led Davidson to inquire as to why he did not also write in French. Conrad's reply was immediate: "To write French you have to know it. English is so plastic—if you haven't got a word you need you can make it, but to write French you have to be an artist like Anatole France."[3] It is a line whose enigma I periodically attempt to assess. Having settled in France, Davidson was utterly won over by the manor in Touraine as soon as he saw it. "Bécheron," he wrote, "had a beautiful gray façade and I was fascinated by its pigeon tower. The house was enclosed by old stone walls, and on the opposite side of the road there was a vegetable and flower garden. From its terrace you looked out over the lovely valley of the gently flowing Indre" (208).

The landscape of the commune of Saché had, in a previous century, already attracted the attention of another artist intent on portraying the full range of his age. Balzac, approaching the town from the neighboring village of Azay-le-Rideau, wrote in *Le Lys dans la vallée*, which is set in Saché: "I climbed to a ridge and for the first time admired the château d'Azay . . . and, then, in a hollow, I saw the romantic walls of Saché, that melancholy abode, full of harmonies too solemn for superficial people, but dear to poets whose soul is in mourning. Thus it was, in the years to come, I grew to love its silence, its great wizened trees, and the mysterious aura that pervades its solitary vale."[4] Balzac, the fictive historian of the society of his day, had lived in the château on one side of the Indre, where he wrote *Le Père Goriot* and *Louis Lambert*. Davidson, who thought of himself as the "plastic historian" of his age, set up shop on the other—all in a commune whose population is currently listed as little more than a thousand.

My connection to this world, the absoluteness of whose distance from my middle-class childhood in New York is hard to imagine in an age of mass air travel, was by way of an act of generosity. Jo Davidson had two sons, one of whom, Jacques, was living in New York with his family, where, for one reason or another, he was having trouble making ends meet. My understanding is that my parents, and perhaps above all my grandmother, the founder of Melnikoff's, the local dry goods store which she operated for about half a century, had been particularly kind in extending credit to Jacques's wife, Elisabeth, an interpreter at the United Nations. A debt of gratitude was incurred. In addition, my grandmother, whose way of holding court to all and sundry in the store had a number of locals dubbing her the "mayor of Yorkville," the neighborhood in which the store was located, was the kind of individual who would have appealed to Zabeth, as she was known. There was, that is, a bond of affection as well.

In 1952, not long after the publication of his memoir, Jo Davidson, at age sixty-eight, was finally felled by the last of his heart attacks. His had been an extraordinary life, surrounded by eminence. In his later years, his career as a sculptor, which brought him into compacted but intense contact

with so many of the world's celebrities, fused with an odd political vocation. An early supporter of Franklin D. Roosevelt, he hitched his wagon
to the waning political star of former vice president Henry A. Wallace,
whom the Democratic Party had replaced in 1944 with Harry S. Truman.
Davidson was allied with the left wing of the party, becoming chairman
of the Independent Citizens' Committee of the Arts, Sciences and Professions, an embryonic political action committee supportive of Wallace. By
1946, *Time* was describing him as "a political leader of considerable stature"
and placed his portrait on the cover of its September 9 issue. The caption
read: "Sculptor Jo Davidson, Amateur Politician: In Paris, the left bank; in
Hollywood, the left wing."[5] Having been asked by a grateful FDR whether
the press had started calling him a Communist yet, he may nonetheless
not have been prepared for the right-wing venom subsequently unleashed
against him.

There was an odd precedent for Davidson's suffering at the hands of
the right-wing press. As a young man he had headed off, accompanied by
a poet friend and one of his sculpting models, to visit Upton Sinclair's socialist colony at Helicon Park in New Jersey. When it turned out that the
colony did not have beds for them, they were forced to leave, turned out
into the wintry cold. The next day's *Evening Sun* was all too happy to headline the naiveté of the expedition, and perhaps the heartlessness of their
"socialist" hosts as well: "POET, SCULPTOR AND LADY OUT IN THE COLD,
COLD WORLD" (32). What strikes me as most uncanny is Davidson's evocation of the friend, Sadakichi Hartmann, Nagasaki-born, half-German,
thoroughly Americanized *fin de siècle* aesthete and trickster: "Sadakichi was
brought up in Germany by Paul Haise and then in France under the tute-
lage of Stéphane Mallarmé, the French poet. He finally landed in Boston
where Mrs. Jack Gardner took him up" (28). Others have commented on
the fascination of Sadakichi Hartmann, of whom Ezra Pound once commented: "If one hadn't been oneself, it would have been worthwhile being
Sadakichi."[6] But it is the short circuit between Mallarmé and Boston, the
metonymy of a life not merely his, which gives me pause . . .

*

Not the least remarkable part of Jo Davidson's life had been the sixteenth-century manor in Saché. After the war, Davidson, aware of the burden of keeping the property up, toyed with the idea of selling it. But his

numerous friends, who had enjoyed the hospitality of the extrovert sculptor, were horrified at the prospect and, according to his memoir, proposed the organization of a society of Friends of Bécheron. Each would contribute a membership fee for the privilege of coming to visit in Bécheron—on the condition that the Davidsons themselves would be there (350). That plan never got off the ground, but it is tempting to think of the later fate of Bécheron as having its roots in that project. Jacques and Elisabeth Davidson, not long after the sculptor's death, opted to move to France, to Bécheron, which they set up as a hotel of the *chambre d'hôte* variety. Those were the years when one could more or less choose one's guests (among the moneyed Americans discovering postwar France), and the Davidsons did so with an eye to retaining the conviviality the manor had enjoyed during the decades the sculptor had spent there. A number of Davidson's busts were transferred to the lower level of the Balzacian château across the Indre, where they formed a permanent exhibit. Meals were served at the manor by the chef—no, the cook—to guests in a splendidly rustic dining room overlooking the valley of the Indre. (It was one of the maxims of the house that a good cook would add ten years to your life, while a good chef would take ten years off it.) Television was nowhere to be found. After dinner, guests would retire to the drawing room for conversation. It was a faintly archaic ambiance of the sort that had already disappeared in the United States and would not last that much longer in France.

Among the guests that the Davidsons invited, out of gratitude for the numerous favors they had received at Melnikoff's, the family shop, were my parents. Working as they did from 9 a.m. to 9 p.m. six days a week (except for an early closing on Tuesday nights, devoted principally to watching the slapstick of Milton Berle on television), they were in no position to accept the invitation. Ah! But they did have a son, then approaching sixteen, who was studying French as a foreign language in school and indeed seemed to have a talent for it. In short order, an arrangement was concocted: I would spend the summer of my junior year in high school, 1960, at Bécheron, as an elder companion to Laurent, the Davidson son, but also as someone who would keep the children of the assorted guests happy, a counselor of sorts, were it not ludicrous to think of Bécheron in any way as a summer camp. What this amounted to was taking visiting children on biking treks from château to château—*d'un château l'autre,* as the novelist put it—in the Loire valley.

There were other delights. Jacques's younger brother Jean had moved into the mill just down the river, where he lived with his wife, the daughter of Alexander Calder, who was also part of the household. (I have the distinct recollection of the top-heavy Calder, looking somewhat tipsy and stretching out his arms, a bit like one of his mobiles, to keep his balance while making his way across the garden.) My six weeks in Bécheron were, altogether, an experience so eye-opening that when I was asked, about a year later at Harvard, what I wanted to major in, it was clear to me that the answer was the summer of 1960. Which translated, in the jargon of Harvard, into "French History and Literature."

*

Was there an underside to my season in paradise? No doubt. When I think of that first night in France, of my daze amidst the elegantly angled cigarette holders at what turned out to be Jacques Davidson's fiftieth birthday party, I am suddenly reminded of the circumstances of my trip. Shortly before my nervously anticipated departure to France, my father was hospitalized on an emergency basis. Was it a heart attack? Or one of his serial hernia operations? My father insisted that I not miss the trip, although it was clear that he could not drive me to the airport. That task fell to an uncle, who, I later learned, had long been suspicious of the bookishness of this son of his sister Frances. The date of the trip, at the tail end of June, moreover, coincided with my parents' wedding anniversary. Viewed in a certain light, the incapacitation of my father and my own flight to France on my parents' anniversary made perfect sense. Will France have been my major transgression?

The flight was considerably delayed, indeed jeopardized, by an Air France strike. The result was that my host, Jacques Davidson, would be unable to come to Paris to pick me up at Orly, since I would be arriving shortly before his birthday celebration. All this I discovered upon arriving in Paris. A call to Bécheron clarified the situation, and I was relieved to receive instructions and make my way to the Gare d'Austerlitz and a train that would take me to a station outside Tours, where I was awaited by the dapper celebrant, decked out in formal garb, of his half century on the planet. Whereupon we headed in his *deux-chevaux* to the manor, so far from the mercantile clutter of the store on Eighty-fourth Street I had just left, to the elegantly angled cigarette holders and the party. Of such nights are family romances born.

There is—or may have been—more. I am suddenly reminded of a humiliation, fairly typical of early adolescence, experienced during one of the summers I spent in a camp in the Berkshires. It was during one of the awkward events called socials, where boys from Camp Potomac and girls from Camp Wahconah were invited to "socialize," decorously, while dreaming of less decorous encounters. That evening I found myself locked in conversation with one of the most attractive girls in the group, a pert brunette I had been eyeing for days. The pleasure of her company was compounded by its unexpectedness, since our prolonged encounter at the social seemed to violate an implicit rule of engagement. In a word, it was assumed that the attractiveness of girls would be matched to the athletic prowess of the boys. And since my childhood in Manhattan had given me little access to the ball fields (and Little League teams) of the suburbs, baseball, in sum, was not my forte. (During the annual awards ceremonies at the camp, I was regularly given the medal for "character," plainly a consolation prize.) Still, there was the small miracle of that evening, followed, no doubt, by my all too vocal crowing of my success, the palpable annoyance of my bunkmates at what seemed to them a disruption in the way things were meant to be, and, finally, by a humiliating return to reality. Now, my reason for recounting this episode is that the day before leaving Saché, I discovered, inadvertently, that the (emphatically Jewish) name of the girl in question happened to be a precise anagram of the words "Manoir de Bécheron."

The entire episode, however trivial, leads me to wonder about its connection to the enchantment of that summer, and of all that ensued from it. It is as though, at some unperceived level, the Francophile passion spoke to—or enacted (at what distance from the "self-assurance," so daunting to its best readers, of my first book?)—an experience of humiliation overcome. A second case springs to mind. During the heyday of television quiz shows (with their attendant scandals), a period long forgotten but recently recalled to public awareness by a popular film, word reached the corporate trust around Jack Barry, a customer in my parents' shop and sometime master of ceremonies of the soon-to-be-infamous *Twenty-one*, that the shopkeepers' bookish young son might just be a suitable contestant. (The famous "Quiz Kids" program was about to go off the air, but a surrogate show was envisaged.) I recall my mother bringing me down to corporate headquarters on Madison Avenue and being told to wait outside as I was subjected to a battery of quizzes. The results were deemed acceptable enough for me to be invited back for a second interview, on which occasion I would be questioned on a specific area of expertise. I chose to be quizzed on geography. When I next showed up, I was escorted into the boardroom and told, to my shock, that I would be quizzed on what was deemed my area of specialty, which was opera, a subject about which I knew next to nothing. The results, disastrous, were no surprise to me, and I was gently led out of the room and thanked for "dropping by." My fiercely protective mother, when she found out what had happened, protested the exploitation of her child but proved no match for the Madison Avenue staff members.

The results of that misencounter with the world of television were twofold. On the one hand, I emerged with a clear sense of how potentially corrupt the world of quiz shows was, and more specifically how the corruption might function. Once the staffers discovered, through the battery of quizzes, what a contestant knew and did not know, it became simple to ask him what he knew if one wanted him to win, and only slightly less simple to stymie him if one wanted him to lose. I was, in sum, not shocked at the scandal when it erupted. On the other hand, I emerged with a need to assuage the gaping wound of my glaring ignorance of opera. And that need soon developed into a full-blown passion for the art. It began with Milton Cross's celebrated volume of opera plots, moved on to a collection of long-playing records, then culminated in a number of Saturday afternoons waiting on line outside the old Metropolitan Opera House on 39th Street for standing-room tickets. (The truly sinister aspect of those waits did not come home to me until a recent viewing of a Diane Arbus retrospective. Her photographs are generally regarded as keys to the freakishness of a certain America. What struck me was to what an extent they are portrayals of the freakishness of the New York City in which I grew up. The imaginary caption of the photo—of me—that Arbus never shot: "Young loner waiting on line for standing-room ticket to the opera.")

Was the passion for opera, then, like the investment in France, a story of humiliation overcome? Might they even, at some level, be the same? A few years ago, I published a piece in an American monthly called "America: The Opera." The theme was vintage Franco-American: the supplanting of Lafayette by Beaumarchais as central French hero of the American Revolution. For between writing *The Barber of Seville* and *The*

Marriage of Figaro, Beaumarchais's principal activity was running guns for the rebels in the American War of Independence. More specifically, the piece toyed with the possibility that it was the scenario of *The Barber*, soon to be the plot of Rossini's *opera buffa*, that informed the actions of the gunrunning playwright during the Revolution. An ingénue, Rosine, slips the bonds of her cruel and crotchety *tuteur*, Dr. Bartholo, to pursue her romance with her suitor, the Count Almaviva, all with the deft assistance of the trickster valet, Figaro. Transpose to the American Revolution, and one has Lord Stormont, the British ambassador to Paris, in the role of Dr. Bartholo; the Count de Vergennes, the French foreign minister, in the role of Almaviva; Beaumarchais himself, with all his ingenious deceptions, in the role of Figaro; and none other than Benjamin Franklin, age seventy, in the role of the ingénue. America's cult of France, in sum, was there at the inception, its Declaration of Independence, as one astute critic put it, nothing so much as an SOS addressed to France. The American cult of France, then, as grand opera, a story of twin humiliations, both intimate and international, overcome.

*

Many years later, on a sweltering August day, I showed up at the door of Bécheron with my wife and two children. I knew that the Davidsons were no longer living there but was eager to see, to share with my family, at whatever distance and however obliquely, whatever of it might be visible. When we discovered there was no one home, we made do with the standard visit to the Balzacian château, disappointed that the "permanent" Jo Davidson exhibit no longer existed. Perhaps these pages have been written to redeem the several disappointments of that visit. The sun was blazing on the deserted village square, which was a blinding white. We sought refuge in the cool of the village church, whose Romanesque distinction, after half a century, seemed unchanged. As we climbed into our car, I caught a glimpse of the only human trace of the Saché that had so affected me: the name of the square, clearly indicated, was now "Place Alexandre Calder."

CITIES

New York/Angoulême

Perhaps the most succinct summary of my trajectory as a critic is one that would take me from a first book, in 1974, intent on bringing home to America, in an English worthy of it, what was then achieving notoriety under the name "French structuralism," to my most recent volume, which concludes with a chapter on the invention of French structuralism in Manhattan during the wartime exile of Claude Lévi-Strauss and Roman Jakobson. What was originally envisaged as an exotic import, it turned out, had in fact been conceived in the city of my birth, and more or less at the same time to boot. In what follows, I move things backward in relation to that scenario: not a French vanguard always already American, but a New York always already haunted by the French city it very easily could have been. As that failure (to be French) comes to lodge at the heart of what one of the city's current monuments calls "Truth," it appears to enact, on the map of America, an allegory of post-structuralism itself.

*

The identification, in 1996, of a Michelangelo boy-with-quiver in the shadows of the lobby of the Cultural Services of the French Embassy on Fifth Avenue was greeted alternately as aesthetic windfall—how resist the curve of the torso?—and multicultural fluke: that a bit of the Florentine Renaissance should have taken up secret residence on French territory in the heart of Manhattan was as weirdly delightful a touch of cultural chaos as New Yorkers had been served in some years.

Yet that very weirdness, New York's Franco-Florentine connection, turns out, upon reflection, to be less a bizarreness attaching secondarily to beauty than a bracing reminder of truth itself. At the southern tip of Manhattan, there is a little-visited—lesser—statue whose inscription informs us that "in April 1524, the Florentine-born explorer Verrazzano led the French caravel La Dauphine to the discovery of the Harbor of New York and named these shores 'Angoulême' in honor of Francis I, King of France." Planted in front of the Verrazzano pedestal is a second bronze—this one of an allegorical figure of Truth pointing with her sword to a book opened to a page on which the date 1524 is inscribed. As though the revisionist unseating of Henry Hudson from his throne as (Anglo-Dutch) discoverer of New York in 1609, the romance of exploration I was taught in grade school, were the very prototype of the exploits or upsets in which Truth revels.

There was something refractory, however, in Truth's Franco-Florentine message. When Averell Harriman, New York's governor, decreed April 17, 1957, to be "Giovanni da Verrazano Day," he departed from the Italian double *z* of the statue's inscription, thus slightly Gallicizing the name of a Florentine who, in his years of residence in Normandy and Lyon, was regularly known as some variant of Jean Vérassen; but he left no doubt as to the true honorees of the holiday: the "fellow-citizens of Italian descent" to whom we are "greatly beholden." As though France were no more than a way station between Florence and New York. Indeed, the statue of the explorer at the tip of Manhattan was originally an Italian gift offered in 1909 in cordial protest of the tricentenary celebrations of Henry Hudson's discovery. So that, if the Truth of Henry Hudson 1609 is the Florentine Verrazzano 1524, as the statue suggests, the truth of that Truth is that the entire American "career" of the explorer was spent in the service of France. The Fifth Avenue Michelangelo, that is, with its yoking together of the French and the Florentine, has the quirky coherence of a residue—a displaced trace of a forgotten origin. Let us pause then, in these days when the waning or downsizing of French glory has become the bitterest of bromides, when not even the Speaker of the House could prevail, in 1997, on his ranks—more indifferent than outraged—to attend a joint session of Congress addressed by then French president Jacques Chirac, to reflect, if only toponymically, on the Gallic world that might have been ours.

New York, it appears, would have been Angoulême, after François's title of nobility—François d'Angolesme—before ascending the throne. It was a tradition that continued on maps long enough for the first French denomination of tobacco—long before Jean Nicot, who gave us "nicotine," brought the stuff back from Lisbon to Paris in 1561—to be *herbe angoumoisine*: the Angoulême weed. The harbor of New York was named Sainte-Marguerite after the king's sister, the future Marguerite de Navarre. New Jersey became the Lorraine coast (after a prominent French cardinal), the Delaware River, Vendôme (after the duke of that name), and Cape Cod, long before Champlain called it Cap Blanc in 1604, Cap Pallavicino (after a Florentine captain who would die in François's army at Pavia). The whole region, inevitably, would be called "la Francescane" in honor of the king.

When Verrazzano returned to Dieppe, his trip was regarded a failure. The closest he came to mineral wealth were the sweet potatoes whose color, it was hoped, might be regarded as proof of copper deposits. And the major objective of finding a route to Cathay or the eastern shore of India had plainly not been attained. It was in the interest of all concerned—the other colonial powers and the embarrassed French—to let Verrazzano's financially disastrous voyage slip into oblivion. (Jacques Habert, the leading French expert on the explorer, reminds us that as late as 1864, Buckingham Smith, president of the New York Historical Society, was denouncing the whole Verrazzano tradition as rooted in fabrication.)[1] The only enduring legacy was a couple of place names floated on the map of the New World. Maryland was sufficiently delightful to merit the name "Arcadie." Stripped of its *r*, the name would float northward to designate, eventually, Canadian Acadia. Block Island—or was it Martha's Vineyard?—was compared in size to the island of Rhodes in Verrazzano's report to the king. No need to insist on what label that metaphor apparently settled into once maps were stabilized.

Yet if the Florentine's expedition of 1524 constituted the "truth" of Hudson's voyage almost a century later, and if French sponsorship were the truth of that truth, the most haunting legacy of Verrazzano's travels remains a mirage at the center of that latter truth. Observing the Chesapeake from what is now Cape Hatteras, the explorer was convinced he was looking onto the "Eastern Sea" that would take him to Cathay and beyond if only a suitable passage to its waters could be found. The cartographical tradition of that ocean dividing what is now the United States remained intermittently alive throughout the sixteenth century. Walter Raleigh, who colonized Virginia in 1587, did so after setting out in quest of what had come to be known as the Verrazzano Sea. Meanwhile the crucial waterway to the East, the illusion motivating Verrazzano's journeys, had itself begun to float northward. Might it not be that "Lake of Angoulesme" which appears on an English map for the last time in 1625: a massive body of water in what is now New York State, joining up with the Saint Lawrence River and enabling the fabled journey to the East? But the Hudson went only so far . . . Finally, the Verrazzano Sea, the mirage at the heart of "truth," having migrated upward to the equally fantastic Lake of Angoulesme, came quite simply to coincide with the actual contours of the lake that did indeed join up with the Saint Lawrence, our present-day Lake Ontario.

The upshot? For those stunned by the odd paths through which truth and mirage come to negotiate the compromise we agree to call reality, and even more that such a negotiation should literally have provided the ground on which we tread, the Franco-Florentine connection assumes exemplary status. More than an exemplum of beauty, the Fifth Avenue Michelangelo is an idiosyncratic reminder of the "origins" of New York, a path of access to the bizarre confection of truth. Perhaps the statue, on loan to the Metropolitan Museum of Art, should be returned forthwith to its original Gallic haunt.

4

Boston/Vichy

The idealism of adolescence, in its kitsch exuberance, typically, in my case, chose—or fantasized—the struggle between the Resistance and the Nazis, good and evil, as its exemplary contest. Years later, once the French themselves had become resigned to the fact that theirs had been a war fundamentally blemished by the lures of collaboration, the heroic posture was taken up, on the cheap, by many an American journalist, who implicitly affirmed—or fantasized—his or her own moral superiority by lamenting a France that had never "come to terms" with its sorry past. It is the city I have lived in for a quarter of a century, Boston, which afforded me an opportunity to challenge such moral exhibitionism by relating the career of a superstar of Nazi-occupied Paris, who made the transition to being a cultural icon of Boston without missing a beat. Shortly after the piece appeared, it was the subject of a somewhat tendentious reading by the columnist Alex Beam in the Boston Globe. His column, in turn, provoked a response by an intimate of the icon in question, which I first learned about at a university banquet when my employer, the president of Boston University, took me aside and asked me whether I had ever heard of one Mrs. S***, the author of the response. When I answered in the negative, he responded, not without relish: "Well, she says you're a God-damned liar in this morning's Globe." At the end of this chapter, I append my reply to Mrs. S***.

*

The French, according to one of the more enduring commonplaces of American journalism, have never managed to come to terms with their complicity in the Nazi-spawned horrors of World War II. It is a notion which, like many another *idée reçue*, suffers less from untruth than from anachronism. Ever since de Gaulle's withdrawal from the political stage in 1969, and no doubt in part in order to ensure the permanence of that withdrawal by blemishing the "resistencialist" myth around which his eminence was built, the French have all but wallowed in their sense of collective guilt in relation to the genocide of the "dark years." Explanations may vary, but few serious observers can doubt that the French, for decades now, have indulged in a specific form of traumatophilia that its most prominent chronicler, Henry Rousso, on the model of the "Vietnam syndrome" (and curiously contemporary with it), has called the "Vichy syndrome." From Marcel Ophuls's filmed indictment "Le Chagrin et la pitié" to the scandal of Mitterrand's belatedly acknowledged—and ongoing—ties with one of the more prominent villains of the Vichy regime and beyond, the French intelligentsia and its readership en masse have all but luxuriated, at a time of diminishing French presence on the world scene, in affirming France's central presence, *albeit on the wrong side*, in what all agree must be the principal catastrophic event of the twentieth century. Indeed, the tendency has been so marked that it has provoked a backlash among the very intelligentsia originally associated with the tendency. Rousso, the original chronicler of French ambivalence toward coming to terms with the Vichy period, has since warned of the "perverse effect" of maintaining a "Judeocentric" view of the French experience of World War II.[1] The philosopher Alain Finkielkraut, the author of the most insightful analysis of Holocaust denial in France (and above all in a fringe of the French left), has since come to lament a kind of hyperesthesia toward spurious cases of anti-Semitism, the degeneration of the *notion* of Holocaust denial into any refusal to entertain the ludicrous belief that the French republic itself is fundamentally afflicted with a kind of "simmering Nazism."[2] Pierre-André Taguieff, an analyst of racism whose analyses, at their most devastating, have targeted the blind spots of antiracism itself, has taken to citing a tag of Leo Strauss, *reductio ad Hitlerum*, in his most recent critique of the (presumably absurd) inability of the French intelligentsia to see anything but the genocide in every subject to which it turns its attention.[3] If we may judge, in sum, from recent statements of Rousso, Finkielkraut, and Taguieff, the French have come full circle, and are now—or have, until recently, been—in a period of what might be called anti-anti-anti-Semitism, a tendency to put a halt to a series of deformations in understanding born of the beneficent but belated combat against the extreme case of a particularly odious prejudice. The double (in fact triple) negative of our formulation—anti-anti-anti-Semitism—has its own logic, of course, and though it would be wrong to allow the double negative to cancel itself out, it would be naive to overlook the logical and semantic affinities of that unwieldy label with anti-Semitism itself. The American journalistic cliché, that is, in its anachronism, runs the risk of being just anachronistic enough not to be completely wrong.

One of the more insightful manifestations of the Vichy syndrome was *L'Etat culturel: Essai sur une religion moderne*, a book-length polemic published in 1991 by France's preeminent literary historian, Marc Fumaroli, against the cultural policies of the Mitterrand regime. Fumaroli, a Tocquevillean liberal, lashed out against the government's mind-numbing will to inundate the French public, at every available street corner, with some state-sponsored cultural manifestation or other, and visited on his reader the surprising revelation (or claim), years before Mitterrand's own Vichy links were a matter of public notoriety, that the true ancestor of the cultural policies of the Socialist Party, then in power, was the Vichy regime. From which demonstration I shall adduce a specific example. The "brutal pathos" of national-socialist pageantry, the author argues, was a matter of emulation for the National Revolution in France, and one of the principal manifestations of Vichy's effort to catch up with its fascist neighbors on the mass-cultural front was a series of four grandiose fêtes, including a Fête du Travail, featuring a parade of French peasants, in "accordance with the principal directives of the National Revolution," a series of simultaneous spectacles performed on five platforms spread over a field, a text adapted from Hesiod's *Works and Days*, and an original score by Marcel Landowski conducted by Charles Münch.[4] Here, according to Fumaroli, was the ancestor of that state-sponsored "will to culture" that would make its subliminal way, via the Gaullist ministry of André Malraux, to the bicentennial bashes of 1989 that became signature manifestations of the Mitterrand regime.

At this point, the American reader, and specifically the Bostonian I have become, takes pause. Charles Munch, who succeeded Koussevitsky as chief conductor of the Boston Symphony in 1949 and continued in that post until 1962, is widely known as one of the glories of American musical performance. In that role, according to the *New Grove Dictionary*, he pursued a policy of making the BSO "the chief agent for the introduction of new French music to the American public," a policy that had been initiated in the 1920s by the orchestra's then director, Pierre Monteux.[5] And in between the two phases of Gallic glory on the Charles, one might ask (or infer) from Fumaroli's mention, might Munch have served an apprenticeship as musical propagandist for Pétain's National Revolution?

*

(And here the memoirist in me would interpolate: Boston, before it was a city, or even the name of a university, was for me, first of all, and from the time of my childhood, the name of a symphony orchestra. Growing up with a brother gifted with perfect pitch, I was perhaps slated to see music trump everything else, take on a touch of the sacred. My brother was primary officiant in that domestic cult, my own genius loci, working miracles at the keyboard from as early as I remember. Years later, I would buy a small upright for my daughter with the down payment I received for a translation of Bredin's history of the Dreyfus affair. It was then that I realized how deeply the cult of music had affected me. To translate, page by page, at that old Kaypro keyboard became my silent response to the sight-reading skills of my pianist brother, a talent that I could never hope to match.

Why, though, was it Boston that became the cult's principal shrine? It was by way of Tanglewood, the summer home of the Boston Symphony Orchestra in western Massachusetts. For it was there, during a 1950s summer, that I would make my weekly pilgrimage, hitchhiking from the summer camp on Lake Pontoosuc, during my weekly day off, to Tanglewood to hear my brother perform with the Boston Symphony, in the festival chorus, under the legendary baton of Charles Munch. To each the Bayreuth he can afford . . . My thrill was such that years later, there are still fragments of those concerts ringing in my ears, stray percussive bits of Poulenc's Gloria; a line, sung against a throbbing string accompaniment, from Berlioz's Roméo et Juliette ("se découvre à Juliette"); and finally the orgasmic conclusion of Ravel's Daphnis et Chloé. All French, I now realize, and all fairly erotic. Such were the elements of one adolescent's thrilled assimilation, almost in the flesh, of what the New Grove Dictionary *referred to rather dryly as Munch's effort to introduce French music to the American public.)*

*

A first search for an answer to the dilemma suggested by the passage from Fumaroli's polemic took me to Munch's memoir of 1954, published by Editions du Conquistador (Paris), under the title *Je suis un chef d'orchestre*. It is a volume as elliptical on matters political as it appears expansive on matters musical. Consider the conductor's evocation of World War I. He had only recently gone off to Paris to study violin under the eminent virtuoso Lucien Capet when war was declared: "1914 . . . the war. I returned to Strasbourg by the last train to cross the blue line of the Vosges. As soon as hostilities had ceased, after four years away from music, its festivities and its works, the best job I could find was an extremely modest position in an insurance company."[6] The reader assents without difficulty to the notion that the Great War might place a crimp in any musical career. But Munch's situation was in some ways unique. Munch's? Fumaroli had referred to the performance by Münch, and the *New Grove* entry is for "Münch [Munch], Charles (*b* Strasbourg, 26 Sept 1891; *d* Richmond, VA 6 Nov 1968). French conductor and violinist." For French though he might be, Strasbourg, his place of birth, had been German since the Franco-Prussian War. The future champion of French music, that is, had abruptly left Paris and his dreams of musical glory in order to take up arms against France: "as a resident of Alsace he was conscripted into the German army for war service, 1914–18." So the lapidary quality of Munch's own mention of his war years would appear to evade consideration of a dilemma, encapsulated in the twin spellings of his name, exquisite in its ramifications. The *New Grove* itself, however, seems evasive when compared to the evocation of Munch's war years in *Baker's Biographical Dictionary of Music*: "At the outbreak of World War I (1914), he enlisted in the German army. He was made a sergeant of artillery, and was gassed at Peronne and wounded at Verdun."[7] *Grove's* "conscription," if we are to credit *Baker's*, was in fact enlistment and issued in the agony of gassing at the hands of the allies.

On the subject of World War II, which one finds it hard to imagine as anything other than traumatic for him, Munch seems both evasive and an apologist for evasion: "There were the four terrible years of the German occupation. My role at the time consisted in enabling a kind of mental escape toward more felicitous worlds. I went at it with a fervor that the agony of seeing my country shackled, gagged, and bruised augmented tenfold. No material force will ever be able to break the *élan* of music."[8] The

New Grove mentions that the conductor assumed the directorship of the Société des concerts du Conservatoire de Paris in 1937 and does not even mention World War II. *Baker's* reports that he stayed in his post during the German occupation, and that "refusing to collaborate with the Nazis, he gave his support to the Resistance, being awarded the Légion d'honneur in 1945." All would appear to have resolved itself in time (for the assumption of the leadership of the Boston Symphony a few years later), but it would also appear to leave us with the conundrum of the "Resistance" conductor known—to Fumaroli at least—for his stirring participation in the pageants of the Vichy regime.

The conundrum has been deepened, if not resolved, by the publication of a pioneering collective volume, edited by Myriam Chimènes, under the title *La Vie musicale sous Vichy.*[9] The book is in a series under the general editorship of Henry Rousso, and as such may be situated as part of the general reaction against what has been interpreted as a hypersensitivity in relation to the Jewish question: Rousso begins his preface by ironizing on the naiveté of a 1976 film, *Chantons sous l'Occupation,* whose director, André Halimi, waxed indignant at the very thought of anyone being able to "sing" while the horrors of the genocide were going on. Yet for anyone exercised by the conundrum just evoked, the volume's principal surprise is quantitative in nature. With twenty-seven entries in the index, Charles Munch is one of the two most frequently discussed figures in the collection. For from the professional point of view, the harrowing years of the Occupation were golden years for Munch. Indeed, they appear to have been golden years for classical music in France *tout court.* Jews may have been drummed out of the world of music (and the Conservatoire, in fact, was the only public teaching establishment in metropolitan France from which the totality of Jews were excluded under Vichy); Jewish composers—Mendelssohn, Dukas, Milhaud—may have been banned from performance; and yet there had been a considerable increase in both the number of and attendance at classical concerts in relation to the prewar years.[10] As the principal conductor of the oldest of the major Parisian symphonies, the Société des concerts du Conservatoire, founded in 1828, Munch, whose performances were regularly reviewed enthusiastically by Arthur Honegger (using the spelling Münch) in the collaborationist journal *Comoedia,* was the object of special adulation. In a posthumous volume of homage to her native son, published in Strasbourg in 1992, a statement by Georges Dandelot (cited from the November 2, 1941, issue of *L'Information musicale*) captures the extent of the adulation surrounding Munch (or Münch) during the "dark years" in terms redolent of fascism: "the crowd displays its gratitude to its conductor through its allegiance and an enthusiasm more delirious [*chaque fois plus délirant*] at every turn."[11]

Music, Munch had said in his memoir, offered an escape from the rigors of the day, and one should be willing to credit the enthusiasm he inspired during the war to his ability to satisfy just such an apolitical demand. Moreover, the pageant, with music by Landowski conducted by Munch, that Fumaroli adduced does not even make its way into the recent volume. Yet the book contains two references to Munch during the Vichy years that may give us pause.

The first deals with what was perhaps the most elaborate of the new works commissioned by the government and performed with considerable success, under Munch's baton, in wartime Paris: Alfred Bachelet's symphonic cantata *Sûryâ*. Bachelet, long since forgotten, had been a contemporary of Debussy's at the Conservatory. Indeed, an earlier sketch of *Sûryâ* had been erroneously attributed to Debussy when classified at the Bibliothèque nationale.[12] During the war, he served as honorary president of the musical section of the Groupe Collaboration, so that performance of his work was sure to be ideologically marked in any event. Moreover, the Munch premiere of the piece was accompanied by a choral concert version of the Grail music from *Lohengrin*, in arrangements first presented in 1936 at Bayreuth under Furtwängler's direction. The link with the Reich's favorite composer was intended to be apparent. *Sûryâ* was to be France's response to Wagner. Years earlier the question of the proper French response to Wagner had been opened by the founding of the legendary *Revue wagnérienne* by Edouard Dujardin, whose invention of stream of consciousness would make of him a principal inspiration of Joyce, and Houston Chamberlin, whose speculations on Aryan superiority would make of him a principal inspiration of Hitler. It was a question that Mallarmé, in the first issue of the *Revue*, had deepened in a legendarily ambivalent "rêverie" on the German composer. Here, under Munch's baton, Bachelet and the Société des concerts du Conservatoire were offering something of an ecstatic answer. *Sûryâ* was subtitled "Hymne védique" and was a setting of the first of the nineteenth-century Parnassian master Leconte de Lisle's *Poèmes antiques*. But the Vedic reference was by implication a nod in the direction of Aryanism. The poem following *Sûryâ* in Leconte de Lisle's collection, "Prière védique pour les morts," was in fact inspired by a funeral chant gleaned from Adolphe Pictet's two-volume *Les Origines indo-européennes ou les Aryas primitifs*. (The chant, moreover, had been borrowed from a work by Max Müller, the very thinker whose disquisition on the solar inspiration of Indo-European mythology had so inspired Mallarmé himself.)[13]

    Sûryâ itself is a solar poem and has been diversely interpreted as a recollection of "a morning beneath the tropical sun on the shores of the Indian Ocean" and a "symbol of the course of an individual life."[14] Which it may indeed be. But in the charged atmosphere of Paris 1942, the most eloquent lines of the poem are surely those forming its conclusion. A resplendent warrior bestrides the heavens, dispensing his beneficence on a people who pray to him:

Roi du monde, entends-nous, et protège à jamais
Les hommes au sang pur, les races pacifiques
Qui te chantent au bord des océans antiques!

The Sun is hailed as a warrior, that is, who protects the "peaceful" and "pure-blooded" races who submit to him. But whatever the valence of Leconte de Lisle's configuration as originally conceived, in the context of Bachelet's cantata of 1942, it must have figured as an ecstatic allegory of Vichy's foreign policy: France as the peaceful and submissive protectorate of the warrior king whose benevolence is conditional on the purity of blood (or race) of those who would thrive in his light. And the reaction to Munch's performance seems to have been positive across the board. Paul Landormy greeted it as a "magisterial work, one of the most beautiful to have appeared in France since the war."[15] In *L'Information musicale* of May 8, 1942, Tony Aubin saluted Bachelet as "one of the most authentic and eminent musical personalities of our time," indeed as "one of the primary pillars of the spiritual bridge linking the glorious shores of the past to the uncertain banks of the future."[16] And Honegger himself would weigh in with the following evaluation of the performance in *Comoedia* (April 18, 1942): "This work, magnificent in its lyrical flight, imbued with impressive stylistic unity, a broad and glorious sweep, was given the warmest of receptions. The choruses of Yvonne Gouverné were excellent and Ch. Münch conducted the ensemble with passion and precision."

Sic transit gloria mundi . . . The total oblivion into which the name of Bachelet has fallen, combined with the ecstatic reception accorded his government-commissioned cantata in 1942, offers something of a confirmation of our reading. A work so precisely attuned to the tragically idiosyncratic juncture in history at which France found itself would have been all but *inaudible*, whatever its musical merits, in an era intent on putting that juncture behind it.

There is, however, a second reference to Munch in *La Vie musicale sous Vichy* that merits particular consideration. Earlier we mentioned that Munch was one of the two names most frequently cited in the volume. The other was Alfred Cortot, and it is in the context of a discussion of the wartime career of that distinguished pianist and conductor that the reference occurs. As of May 1942, Cortot, an ardent *pétainiste*, served as technical advisor to the cabinet of Abel Bonnard, minister of national education in the Laval government. As such, Myriam Chimènes has observed, he was not only the only musician but the only artist to take on official responsibilities during the Vichy years.[17] (He was inclined to flaunt his attitude on the understanding that, as a serious musician, he had been engaging in Franco-German collaboration at the highest level for forty years.)[18] In June 1942, he would go to Berlin to perform the Schumann Concerto with the Philharmonic under Furtwängler. In sum, he was one of the more visible Parisian collaborators and would pay for it following the war. After the liberation of Paris, the Société des concerts du Conservatoire refused to accompany him; an official inquiry ruled on April 28, 1945, that there were a sufficient number of extenuating circumstances to keep him out of jail, but administrative sanctions were unanimously recommended, and Cortot was obliged to take up residence in Switzerland in 1947. In his posthumously published *Journal inutile*, Paul Morand comments on the extent to which Cortot, in 1974, continued to be "detested." After he bequeathed a Renoir portrait of Wagner to the Louvre, his adopted son was horrified to see that the frame with the mention "Gift of Alfred Cortot" had been removed.[19] Now, Cortot's crowning achievement as a collaborator was arguably the establishment by law of a Comité professionnel de l'art musical et de l'enseignement libre de la musique. Cortot himself was named chair of the committee—which came to be known as the Comité Cortot—by decree of December 30, 1943, and presumably became Vichy's official music czar as a result. The committee itself was divided into a variety of administrative sections, of which the commission on "orchestras, choruses, and musical societies" was under the direction of Charles Munch[20]—which would, of course, make Munch something of a collaborator himself, for things appeared to be going swimmingly between Munch and Cortot during the war years. A letter from the pianist dated October 13, 1943, begins "Cher et grand Charlie . . ."[21]

But Munch, we have noted, emerged from the war with the Légion d'honneur in 1945. How might one reconcile that fact with what we have been able to infer from the new collective volume? The sole trace of an accusation against Munch that I have encountered is in the form of a refutation penned by Honegger in a letter of 1945. The subject is a series of statements made by the conductor Paul Paray. Paray, who had been conductor of the Orchestre des concerts Colonne when the war broke out, had resigned from that position rather than submit a list of "Israelite" musicians to the authorities. He was able to resettle as principal conductor of the Monte Carlo Opera. In May 1942, a concert he was scheduled to conduct in Lyon, the day after a concert by a German orchestra, turned into a Resistance demonstration—with Paray, in tears, ordering his musicians: "Stand up! La Marseillaise in B-flat!"[22] After the war the Resistance's favorite conductor would gradually make his way to Detroit—even as Munch, a superior performer, would come to settle in Boston. Here, however, are Honegger's epistolary comments on Paray just after the war: "I don't envy you . . . the arrival of Paul Paray, a virtuoso conductor but a professional slanderer. He returned here with a reputation as a 'grand résistant' and immediately began his attacks, public speeches, against Munch, whose success he could not tolerate and whom he could not forgive for having been called to London before he was. Things went as far as an accusation of libel, which resulted in his issuing a retraction and offering an apology."[23] Honegger himself was vulnerable, both for his publications in *Comoedia* and for his participation as part of the French delegation to the Nazi-sponsored festivities in Vienna surrounding the sesquicentennial of Mozart's death.[24] In the euphoria of liberation, however, with Munch conducting "La Marseillaise" to ecstatic crowds in both Paris and his native Strasbourg, no accusation would stick.[25]

At this point, however, we may want to take pause and wonder under what conditions Munch/Münch could *not* have been a collaborator. A

French-speaker born in what was technically the German city of Strasbourg, he headed off to Paris to pursue his career just before World War I,
only to take up arms as an artillery officer against the French, who would
wound him at Verdun and gas him at Peronne. Yet it was against that traumatic backdrop that he opted for French citizenship immediately after the
war, only to head directly for Germany—first Berlin, then Leipzig, where
he served as concertmaster of the Gewandhaus Orchestra—to launch his
career. One begins to suspect that some form of Franco-German collaboration during World War II may, alas, have been a psychical prerequisite to
any form of mental stability. Unless, of course, his music were born of the
very instability embodied by the Franco-German question as it worked its
way through his life.

Nor should we overlook the extent to which fascism may be the
spontaneous ideology of orchestra conductors per se. Shortly after the liberation of Paris, Jacques Chardonne, one of the leading collaborators of literary France, found the metaphor that captured his sense of Hitler's power:
"Intoxicated by music. Leading his people like an orchestra; and, in that
role, incomparable."[26] The sectors of fascist society, functioning harmoni-
ously under the leadership of a beloved chief, would be like the sections
of an orchestra or perfectly integrated ensemble. But Munch himself was
never very far from that metaphor in his evocation of the calling of an orchestra conductor: "But you must also radiate your thought, your capacity for contagion, with enough clarity for the musicians to experience, at
the precise instant you do, the very same desires, thus finding themselves
unable not to express them. You must substitute your will for theirs."[27]
How, we may ask, would a conductor alive to the specificity of his craft
not warm to the affinities of his calling with that of every other *Duce*? As
Chardonne, in his choice of metaphor, may have intuited.

So we are left with a Munch/Münch who—by the geopolitical acci-
dent of his birth, by the special nature of his vocation—could not perhaps
fail to be particularly vulnerable to the allures of "collaboration." Need we
condemn him as such? One of the reasons for the Gaullist "resistencialist"
myth was the intuition that if France were to condemn all of its elites that
were in any way sullied by the tar of collaboration there would be precious
few to assume the elite functions of postwar French society. An economy
of scarcity dictated a measure of indulgence. Now, lest such indulgence
be received as a—small but intolerable—measure of corruption, we may

recall that one of the ongoing scarcities of postwar American society has been a lack of major symphony orchestra conductors. It was under those complex circumstances that the United States, much like France, opted to overlook what we have observed of Munch's career as a collaborator and to take him up as a hero of the American cultural landscape.

Consider that career in the context of the far more sinister story of Klaus Barbie. Barbie, the Nazi "butcher of Lyon," was taken up after the war by the United States Counter Intelligence Corps, which, in a world threatened by Soviet expansionism, recognized in the brutal anticommunist an asset it ought to be willing to pay for. There are, to be sure, no known war crimes attributed to the noncombatant Munch. And it may be argued that the CIA, heir to the Counter Intelligence Corps, was not, perhaps, sufficiently attentive in its reading of the text of *Sûryâ* to realize just what the delirium inspired by Munch's performance of 1942 may have been about; moreover, the conductor's service, brief at best, as head of the orchestral division of the Comité Cortot may have been overlooked. As was, one may suspect, the rousing performance of the Vichy-commissioned pageant, mentioned by Fumaroli, for the Fête du Travail of May 1, 1942. For the sake of music, that supreme art of "evasion," as Munch put it (and there was no greater—or more prominent—conductor in France during the Vichy period), what would one not overlook? In any event, when the CIA, through its front organizations the Congress for Cultural Freedom and the money-laundering Fairfield Foundation, turned itself in the 1950s into America's de facto Ministry of Culture, it knew where to turn. It was Munch who was contacted by Tom Braden, on behalf of the International Organizations Division of the CIA, with the thought of bringing him and the Boston Symphony Orchestra to Paris for a showcase tour. Munch drove a hard bargain, but when the CIA secretly pledged $130,000 (which was listed as a donation from "prominent individuals"), the orchestra was secured.[28] From mainstay of the cultural life of Occupied Paris to showcase of the CIA, with only a few unpleasant accusations by Paray, withdrawn under threat of legal action, in between.

The moral of the story, if there be one, is somewhat elusive—unless that elusiveness itself be the moral. What seems clear is that if France has been unable to come to terms with its Vichy past, as a largely anachronistic journalistic commonplace has it, so, in the idiosyncratic case of Munch, has the United States, and particularly Boston, the city for whom

Munch remains a cultural hero. Somewhere along the line, it should not be forgotten, Munch would have had to submit to the authorities a list of the Jews in his Société des concerts du Conservatoire orchestra, the very Conservatoire, we have seen, that had been uniquely thorough in its practice of de-Judaization. What, one may ask at any juncture of the story, with more or less hypocrisy, would one not do for music? Resignation was an option, as the case of Paul Paray demonstrates, but one not chosen by Munch, who was, by common agreement, the superior conductor. The ex-*résistant* in Detroit never attained the eminence of the sometime collaborator in Boston. At some point the defense may be legitimately raised that feigned collaboration was the subtlest ruse of resistance. But that argument has generally had the disadvantage of making French national honor a function of French hypocrisy. It is to be hoped that the inextricableness of that circumstance, as it came to be lived out in the uniquely vexed case of Charles Munch/Münch, may in some measure have contributed to the most moving symphonic performances in this listener's memory.

*

No sooner do I reread this piece than its affinities with the blood-borne fantasia of the first chapter of this volume close in on me: my brother participant in the cult, at Tanglewood, directed by Munch; his birth on the day before the Germans enter Paris; the hematological complication induced in Frances, my near death as a result . . . But a second date surfaces: March 1, 1894, fifty years to the day before my own birth: Mallarmé delivers his memorable lecture at Oxford on the theme of music as the new ersatz religion and the imperative to resist it—genuine music being found only in les lettres—*in the name of poetry. It was a subject to which I would turn, somewhat naively, in (or as) my Harvard undergraduate thesis on "Mallarmé and Wagner," therein conflating the Franco-German conflict with the resentments of poetry vis-à-vis music, and more soundly, I hope, in my more recent work.[29]*

But what if this entire chapter were but an acting-out in the scholarly press of the fantasy that continues, subliminally, to haunt me? A third date, then: December 22, 1942. The Americans have liberated North Africa; Pétain refuses to leave Vichy; his sympathies become clearer; and Information musicale publishes a glowing review of a concert of "homage" by the Société des concerts du Conservatoire at Vichy, under the direction of Charles Munch, to

Maréchal Pétain, "chef de l'Etat." Pétain had famously made a gift "of his per-
son" to France in 1940. The concert's reviewer thanks Munch "once again" for
the "complete gift of himself" to "our art."

I breathe a sigh of—sad—relief. Might fantasy, in the last analysis, be a
spur (rather than an impediment) to improved scholarship?

Letter to the *Boston Globe*, October 12, 2002

To the editor:

I am impressed by Sylvia S***'s loyalty to the memory of her friend
Charles Munch (Letters, Oct. 11), but less so by her logic. The notion
that in order to find out what Munch was doing in Paris during World
War II, I would have been better off consulting his friends in Boston after
the war, rather than the writings of French historians of the Vichy period, is questionable, to say the least. (What we learn from Alex Beam's
questioning of Roger Voisin, if Voisin's recollections are correct, is that
Munch was capable of misleading his associates as to his wartime activities.) None of the evidence that Sylvia S*** purports to bring to the
Globe—that he was a guest conductor of the Israeli Philharmonic after
the war; that in 1949 Henry Cabot, chairman of the BSO trustees, was
known to be an anti-Nazi; that Munch had a patriotic Alsatian brother-
in-law (!)—is in any way incompatible with what I reported in my article. Which was: that Munch conducted a Vichy propaganda extravaganza
in 1942; that he headed the commission on "orchestras, choruses, and
musical societies" of Vichy's notorious Cortot committee; that as the
conductor of a major Paris orchestra during the war, he would have had
to submit a list of Jewish musicians (for removal). That Munch broke
with Cortot after the war, as Ms. S*** alleges, proves only that the distinguished conductor may have been less loyal a friend than Ms. S***.
Finally, my purpose in the article, which Alex Beam interpreted somewhat tendentiously in his column, was not to present a brief against the
conductor but to gauge some of the ironies surrounding the fact that a
superstar of the cultural scene of Nazi-occupied Paris was able to become
an icon of the cultural scene of postwar Boston without missing a beat.

J. M.

FATHERS

5

Hugo 2000: Fiction

Could he have known English, the old French hero martyred in the first weeks of the Great War? One wanted to believe as much. How else could he, Charles Péguy, have come up with his encomium to the absurd Hugo poem? "Booz endormi," indeed! Victor Hugo once again taking himself for God, this time in the person of Boaz, an elder expert in charity and every other bourgeois grace, and Péguy, the sometime socialist, falling for it! The Biblical boor proud to walk far from every "oblique path," as though poetry itself did not begin with just such a taste for the deviant! No, Péguy, Dreyfusard hero, nonconformist icon, was pulling someone's leg. To have plucked Boaz out of the desert of Hugo's epic silliness and called the piece a "summit" could only have been an exercise in willful perversity, but Péguy now, in the critic, would meet his match. The utter intoxication, *pleine ivresse*, inspired by the poem? Booz was booze, then. Not Boaz asleep—forget the past participle; it was a simple past, a transitive: Booz *endormit*. Booze put you to sleep, and it certainly did, to judge by the effects of a mere glass or two of Merlot with dinner. Already his right lid was drooping; his legs, raised on the stool, were taking on the thickness that, more than any numbness, was the sensation with which his body registered a day too short for the various tasks he would now be too tired to perform.

When the phone rang, it penetrated his daze with the shrillness of an alarm. "August" Boaz, just before fading into the white linen he was proud to wear, took on the ludicrous aspect of those clowns the French call "augustes." Bozo, awake! Not quite "Ridi, Pagliaccio!" but it would have to do as a bridge back to (or was it from?) the concerns of the day. And the voice at the other end. It was his daughter L., recently moved into her exiguous digs at Columbia, about to embark on four years of what the guidance officers called self-fulfillment, and already, he could tell from the tenuousness of tone, something had gone awry. So awful, she implied, to have awakened and found him there, not even knowing him, and his smile of gratitude, or was it triumph? The critic didn't want to hear any more. He was now sick. It had taken so few days for alcohol, the suburban curse, to work its ill. A night on the town, a drink too many, or too daringly mixed, and the horrible prospect of a coupling to her unknown.

The intruder into her room, into their lives, beat a quick retreat. The bureaucracies, police and medical, proceeded to go through their paces, testing blood, powdering surfaces with the blackness from which a print or two might be lifted, indelibly staining the linen into which, with Booz, he had retreated dreamily only minutes before. Booze had put her, still more than him, to sleep, as the poet might have said, and soon it would befall the critic—Bozo, awake!—to make what he could (and before her contemporaries!) of what Victor Hugo seemed preternaturally to know of them both.

Ridi Pagliaccio, then. The lecture would go on (and on and on, if it were a bad day, dead off the tongue, dead to the ear, but on it would go). He knew it would be a risky day, perhaps a painful one, but no, *this* time he would be speaking at just that edge of what he did not yet know that bore a certain promise with it. So when the morning came, he tied his tie, drank his juice, bid his wife good-bye, and took off to regale his small class with the adventures of Boaz asleep. The lineaments of the narrative they could piece together from the poet's alexandrine verse. The grand old widower, whose compulsive charity imbued him with more sex appeal than many a younger man, was some version of Victor Hugo himself. The idea was abroad in the culture at large. A weekly had featured a mod, touched-up photo of the graying author of *Les Miz* on its cover. "Victor Hugo Superstar," as the French caption read, had pink-tinted hair, pink-tinted glasses, and a leather bomber jacket. Far from Boaz's white linens, but no less sexy for that.

Boaz was weird, though. On the Galilean night in question, he had no sooner retired amidst the workers plowing his fields for him than a dream descended from heaven above. Or rather rose from his groin. A genealogical tree, a "Jesse tree" of sorts, as the iconography has it, but which rose from far lower in the anatomy than the burgeoning chest of many a stained-glass fantasy. And all the while, unbeknown to him, young Ruth, for reasons unbeknown even to her, settled by his side, rose beside the cedar, rose drawn to her seeder, before the poet obscured the scene with a Second Empire equivalent of mood music. Boaz aslumber had words only for God, and their sole ambition was to contain in some way the wonder of his erection. David, the minstrel king at the base of his tree, and Christ the dying god at its peak. The redemption of humanity might be effected through orgasm on the condition that it remain autoerotic. She might have sex with him, as a more recent eminence had it, but he must not have sex with her.

The critic began to feel queasy. He had not felt as uncomfortable in years, but now remembered that then too it was in a classroom. Years earlier, he had sat there at the seminar on Freud, exposed to the pounding question of the instructor intent on eliciting from the class grounds for rejecting the latest behaviorist refutation of the Oedipus complex. "Little Hans," the instructor barked, but the class could not make use of his aggressive clue. Meanwhile, the critic began to sweat. As though he had known the answer without quite knowing it. And when the instructor blurted out the only answer that satisfied him—Little Hans, Freud's florid little patient, regularly thought of his mother while masturbating— it came as a humiliation but also a relief. And now the same feeling of extreme discomfort attended his own prodding less of the students than the text, Victor Hugo's protracted silliness of Boaz asleep.

Or booze-induced sleep. So it was the critic who was undergoing L.'s ordeal, sleeping through who knew what, but also inflicting that very ordeal on her. Perhaps a baby boomer (a *harold*-bloomer) *would* want to have it both ways. But he would do his best, Hugo's best, to make amends. At which point a moon rose over his distress. Ruth could feel the injustice of it all, was even willing to let the promised salvation lapse if it were to be purchased at the cost of such humiliation. Her sex with him, not his with her? How American, alas, *was* the great Hugo? He had seen it all. The grand old man strolling in his exile on the Jersey coast had once encountered an island intern, *gardeuse de chèvres*. She blushed; her goats leapt off through the brambles, leaving nothing but a bit of fleece as she disappeared in their wake. Thus the glorious meditation, "Pasteurs et troupeaux." No matter that the poet, in her absence, would rush to fill the void: the true shepherd was the poet, assimilated to the ocean-front promontory as it contemplated the sheeplike waves. All had been triggered and consummated in that fluttering emission of whiteness in an encounter as determinant as it was fleeting. Yes, Boaz was the American epic too, as ludicrous in its new-world postmodern phase as it apparently was in old-world romantic.

Which is why the rising moon exerted its pull, its call to decency and blood on all assembled. The crescent, a scythe in a field of stellar flowers? Let the academics wax lyrical on the joys of a heavenly mirror overarching the earth. What struck the critic, what must have attracted *her*, was the appropriateness of the weapon thrown up by the poem against a poet so vainly tumescent. One swipe and the tree from the groin, brash for a symbol, would crash like a cymbal, putting an end to the slumber of Boaz. He felt sick again. The class, thank God, was over.

The weekend was difficult. A random ride west from his Victorian suburb on Saturday afternoon promised the consolation of a snatch of live opera broadcast from the Met. He was no longer sure he liked opera, which had been a passion of his youth. Perhaps what he enjoyed was a nostalgia for the days in which the high hysteria of it all thrilled him. It was, in this, the only religion he had left. And then, there were the pleasures of remembrance. How long would it take him to identify the opera being performed? The challenge was to see how little time he would need. Not bad, he thought, a religion that can double as a sport. This Saturday, in any event, turned out to be easy. Not only had he tuned in to *Rigoletto*, but there it was: the famous chestnut of an ending. Easy; no, queasy, the same queasiness as the day before in class. Rigoletto, deformed father, opens the sack and discovers to his horror the body of his dying daughter. His hired assassin had chosen her arbitrarily, but it was he, Rigoletto, sublime hunchback, who bore the guilt. A young woman, a daughter, sacrificed, again. And then he remembered that *Rigoletto* was concocted out of a Hugo play. Of course. Verdi's Mantua was translated by his hack librettist out of Hugo's France. Translated? He remembered now that his favorite translator, a Brit, had had a go at the very same play—transported to Scotland this time. The wit of it all was a momentary consolation. How had he winked his way through "La donna è mobile"? "What wenches in French is is *filles*," or some such froth. But the froth this time was more threat than solace. He remembered the fluttering whiteness, the foam, the fleece in the

Jersey bramble just as the intern-shepherdess disappeared. Forget Scotland. Hugo was coming home with a vengeance.

And he thought of the sad spectacle of the American vice president leading the Democratic Convention in the spirited chorus from *Les Miz*. Hugolian uplift! "Do you hear the people sing?" Idealistic fluff. Even the Frenchmen, so influential, so unknown, who put it all together knew better and let one know it. After *Les Miz* came the new *Madama Butterfly*, *Miss Saigon*. The revolutionary dream a scary dance for Asian martinets. And after that, *Martin Guerre*, or the dream of revolution steeped in religious fanaticism at the source. But even their mordant take on the *schwärmerei* that so entranced the vice president packed nothing like the wallop Victor victorious was now visiting on him.

He needed to dispel the mirage, extricate himself, free his daughter from the snare. If he needed the balloon-lift of Hugolian idealism, so be it. Bring on the people; he wanted to hear them sing! He opened his Hugo at random. There it was, the old favorite about the beggar. Watch out! Charity was how old Boaz turned the girls on. They seemed to line up like groupies at a telethon. He wanted a lift out of his nightmare, but a booz-high was what landed him there in the first place. Still this was feel-good Hugo, the clown who made Baudelaire, when he wasn't flattering him, laugh. Give it a try. So the old beggar made his way to the poet's hut, was invited in, and told to shut up. The poet, Promontory Man, was about to contemplate the universe. The beggar's damp cloak, riddled with holes, was stretched out before the hearth. So Victor proceeded to peer and what he saw was the sublime figure of his own charity: *mille trous de lumière*, a thousand points of light. The critic was relieved. Hugo was zeroing in on America again, but had been redirected, as the air traffic controllers say, to Washington. Let him haunt the White House. Who knew? Maybe the vice president, if elected, would appoint him *genius loci*.

And then he saw it. Just before asking the beggar to shut up, he made him an offering, a shimmering bowl of milk. The fleece, the froth, and now the white liquid foam. The man was a psychopath, a serial rapist. Bugger the beggar. He was out of control.

He could not be left alone, would have to be reined in. Monday, his students could see he was under a strain. His bloodshot eyes were as pink as the tinted lenses on the magazine cover. He had decided to proceed in as gingerly a manner as possible, choosing a poem as far from his own apparent interests as he could find. It was time to be academic, unless, as he suspected, it was too late.

The selection this time was from late in the same silly piecemeal epic as had served him up Boaz and his nightmare. It was called "Sultan Mourad." The critic went through the paces. Yes, the sultan was notoriously cruel and the poet was characteristically ironic. Each atrocity earned its mock-honorific epithet. Forget the orientalism; this was a technique the poet had perfected while using Napoléon III, the man who had reduced him to exile in Jersey, as a target. And then he came upon the culminating horror. The sultan took particular pleasure in bricking selected victims into a punitive wall. The critic could tell things were about to shift decisively. He remembered the poet's vision at the beginning of the epic. All those scenes, charged with pathos, like so many high-romantic dioramas, emerging—alive—from a granite wall. So the poet was at some level his own version of Hitler! So be it! It was his business. Let him deal with it.

Later that afternoon, the critic tended to his other class. He was not sure which was more humiliating: to be teaching a French conversation class or to enjoy doing it. It was his first stab at such a course. He remembered the day on which he found out he was going to teach it. He had been asked to put together a few thoughts on "postmodernism" for a pretentious confabulation in one of the more exalted precincts of the university and had approached the task like the jazz improviser he knew he would never be. Hadn't Lévi-Strauss, the dandified anthropologist, made bold to transpose the metaphysics of the great Bergson into the mythology of the Sioux? If so, who was to say—but everyone knew who it was: his friend and colleague the great novelist in a fit of impatience—that it was out of the question that we might one day find a Zulu equivalent of Bergson's cousin, Proust? A nice enough conceit, which was taken a bit more seriously than intended by those at the confabulation. He felt pretentious, tried to defuse matters by suggesting that he had in fact convinced the novelist to be satisfied with a Zulu Zola. Besides, he was aware of the true piquancy of the story. That very morning a colleague, an administrator, had called to say that, alas, enrollment in his Proust class, the *French* Proust, was insufficient to keep the course open. Let the colloquants debate the future probability of a Zulu Proust. He would silently mourn the French one. Postmodernism indeed!

As a result of which it befell the critic to teach an advanced conversation class. It was not an unpleasant experience. Students would bring in articles in multiple copies and he would get them to hold forth on whatever it was in them that they found intriguing. There was the case of the generalized harassment of teachers in the French suburbs—replete with attendant breakdowns. To a student suggestion that what was needed was a town meeting to address the subject, he responded that at such a gathering those in attendance might quickly and disastrously agree that the problem was the number of immigrants in the school. He even found a few pertinent pages in the Parisian novelistic sensation of the year, a talented exercise in nihilism, though whether of a leftist or rightist bent remained unresolved. He brought in the three pages, which presented the interesting hurdle of featuring a few lines of Proust whose excellence a French lycée teacher could find no way to convey to his class. The critic was almost happy to find that he was having a similar lack of success in transmitting a sense of the Proust—in fact, its literal meaning—to his own students. Coherence, even in failure, had its consolations. And then, by the end of the three pages, the lycée teacher himself, in his frustration, had decided to scribble out a racist diatribe to submit to a local vanguard magazine.

The critic's point, in brief, was demonstrated beyond even his audience's capacity to encompass it. But that was an indulgence. Better steer things away from literature. To current events, for example. And thus it was that on the afternoon of the day he had begun teaching Hugo on vicious Sultan Mourad, the very same sultan showed up in the French daily he was combing for articles. Of course, he now realized. At the base of his wall of atrocity, Mourad had etched a tiny dedication to his defeated enemy: "To Vlad . . ." Slavs and Turks. Mourad was the victor in the gigantic battle of Kosovo, a name and site that were now again convulsing the world. Odd, this capacity of the poet to work his way into crisis after crisis of a century he never knew.

The critic's throat was dry. The detour by Washington had over and again proved only that: a detour. He braced himself. The poem seemed vintage Hugo in its silliness. One day, the great villain, out for a stroll, encounters an eviscerated pig, left by its butcher in the roadway, where flies swarm around its gaping wound. The poet seems excited by the wound and its corruption, but so does the sultan. He shoos the flies away from the wound, and moves the dying animal to the side of the road. Whereupon the dying hog lifts its failing lids and casts an ineffable gaze on the sultan before dying. That night the sultan himself dies of a fever contracted while assisting the infected pig. Before the divine tribunal, his kindness ends up counting more than all his atrocities. Salvation is his. Awful! Hitler the loving vegetarian! Victor Hugo, alas! as Gide never tired of saying.

And then the critic noted the terms of the apotheosis. Hugo's elevator is headed straight skyward. Goethe may well be waving as it goes through the roof. The balloon never felt more gaseous. But nothing clicks until Mourad, hero-villain of Kosovo, is lowered into the bejeweled crypt, which gleams like the "insides of an eviscerated beast." Nothing was possible until he entered the wound. It was all there: the chance encounter, the penetration, the ecstatic farewell, and the poetic ascent. Never mind that the order had been changed. Never mind that the encounter was with an animal. The poet had given us the full horror of Kosovo in order to better negotiate and conceal an unspeakable rape. His own.

*

It was shortly thereafter that the critic caused a major polemical stir with a vigorous attack on psychoanalysis and its pertinence to matters literary. He schooled himself frenetically in the positivist tradition whose specialty was pointing out the "screechingly obvious" contradictions in Freud, and he could now screech with the best of them. It was an unexpected development in the otherwise serene critic. But, it was widely noted, he was not without his eccentricities. Who, for instance, would have believed that just last month he had invested that much money in an antique car—and a broken-down Yugo at that?

6

Kandahar 2001: Fact

Kandahar-New York. The local papers marveled at the serendipity that had brought a celebrated playwright not only to cobble together a play set in Afghanistan, and that before the events of the eleventh, but even to come up with a one-liner about the Taliban heading for New York. But Kabul was the city of the play, and compared to the sacred city of Kandahar, it was secularity itself. I had done the playwright one better, then, in that Kandahar was the name sacred to me. That I should be writing this fantasia—but is it?—of Kandahar in New York on a flight from Boston to Los Angeles, the very itinerary of the eleventh, inspires a mild shudder. What it might inspire in my fellow passengers were they to look at this page, written how many thousands of feet aloft, I can only imagine. Happily, my left hand lies over the page; surely no one will read me.

One does not write in order to go unread, however, so allow me to dispel the mystery. Kandahar may be a name sacred to me; it may even be linked, for the New Yorker at heart I remain, to a section of lower Manhattan not far from the site of what would be first the World Trade Center, then Ground Zero. But my Kandahar had nothing to do with religion, or at least with Islam—though it did have a whiff of the transcendent about it. About fifty years ago, my father, eager to reward an overachieving son or perhaps merely to add a dash of style to his otherwise dull wardrobe, took me to a lower East Side sweater wholesaler named Kandahar. As the owner of a dry goods store uptown, he was generally familiar with the turf. His life, it seemed to me, was largely devoted to pleasing others, and the most common form taken by his will to please was the emergency afternoon dash to the lower East Side to find the girdle, bra, or whatever of just the size requested by the customer that morning but, alas, nowhere to be found in the jumble of boxes through which he, or his sales help, would desperately rifle. The item was promised by nightfall (the store closed at 9 p.m.), and thus began the dash downtown. In the hit-and-run descents on Maidenform, Warner, or wherever, I was the lookout. My job was to sit in the double-parked Olds and ward off any cops—with my mere presence, like a pudgy scarecrow—who might be inclined to issue a ticket. It was God-awful boring but managed to leave at least one lasting impression worth noting. WQXR, nothing but the best for this compulsive overachiever, was my one relief from tedium. And particularly Mozart, since I did not yet have the dumb courage to rebel against the boxiness, as Updike put it, of so much classical music, the decorative symmetries that led Shaw to speak of much of what preceded Wagner as so much wallpaper for the ear. So I sat there absorbing Mozart, or rather putting him to use: making him the medium that would allow me to choreograph the chaotic street scene before my eyes into a kind of ballet performed by anxious Jewish wholesalers, indifferent Puerto Rican street vendors, kids in search of a stretch of uncluttered asphalt on which to play ball, and anyone else who might enter the magic of my—that is, Mozart's—ken. All before Peter Sellars even dreamed of setting *Don Giovanni*, was it?, in a New York shooting gallery.

And all the while, I performed my job well. No tickets were issued. Which may have been another reason I was taken that day to Kandahar, where neither my father nor I had ever been before. The sweater I emerged with was a dark green affair, which I wore, and kept wearing for many years after. But my attachment to it had less to do with style than with the circumstances under which it was acquired. When the time came to pay the agreed-on price, the men from Kandahar asked to be excused as they repaired to the back room. When they emerged, it was to inform my father that they had just checked his credit rating in the good book, the Dun & Bradstreet credit guide, and that having ascertained that his rating was "triple A plus," they regarded it a matter of honor—no, of religion—for all concerned that he allow this sweater to serve to initiate his credit account with Kandahar.

Who would have expected that the merchant, an indifferent student for all his youth, should emerge *summa cum laude* from that encounter on the lower East Side? And that he should do so in a kind of surprise cere-mony staged in the presence of his son? It was the green not of Islam but of my father's honor that I wore all those years in the form of a shaggy wool sweater out of Kandahar. I remember sweating later that afternoon as we stopped for a bra on—was it Ludlow Street? A crew of Yeshiva *bukhers*— the phrase is Yiddish for taliban, but who knew?—seemed to prance across the streets to the strains of *Così fan tutte*. I was proud.

*

The fall of Kandahar, my own private Kandahar, did not occur until many years later. It was precipitous and brutal. The circumstance, for all its sadness, was banal. I recount it only for the sake of its bizarre conclusion.

My mother had recently died, and, still grieving, I arrived for the first time with my young family—our daughter was five—at the home above the store on Eighty-fourth Street that my mother's hospitality had graced for so many years. She had died but weeks before.

It was on that occasion that my father brought me into his—their—bedroom, sat me down on what my mother, in a wise gaffe, used to call her "chaise lounge," and informed me that he had taken up with a new woman, none other than my mother's "best friend" of years past, and that he was now considering moving with her to her home in southern Califor-nia. I had returned home in a gingerly effort to reclaim my past, now be-reft of its central presence, and was told that that home was to be dissolved eagerly—and for good. My shock was total. I raised my hands in a gesture of acknowledging the tottering world, the years accumulated, around me, and asked: "And what happens to all this?" Kandahar fell with my father's response: "So that's it. You're only interested in the money." I walked out and, with the exception of one lawyerly visit, did not see him again for the next eight years.

*

A reconciliation of sorts came years later. Children need a grand-father, and the man who would have everything was prepared to put up even with a son who had seen so devastatingly through him in order to have the grandchildren he believed he deserved. And he rose to the occa-sion, with rather spectacular spikes in his grandfatherly skills coinciding with his second wife's first bouts of Alzheimer's. Indeed, it was as though the more she forgot, the more he appeared to remember what I had hoped he would never cease to be. Yet the drama of the fall of Kandahar, as I continued to think of it, continued to simmer beneath the surface. How could he have thought what he pretended to think on that fateful afternoon? It was as though he had staged an imaginary offense in order the better to be able to walk away, to impose on his son the divorce he had never, it appeared to me, had the gumption to ask of his wife, my mother.

Still, that was all speculation. What was needed was less an explanation of his plaint than a refutation. That occasion came my way in the summer of 2001, in my fifty-seventh year, during a visit to the spectacular travertine expanse of the new Getty Center high on the intersecting ridges of two hills north of Los Angeles. With the passage of time, it had become possible to visit the museum, that is, to secure parking without prior reservation. And so it was that on a fine August afternoon, my wife, my father, and I climbed into his 1987 Cadillac and went for a visit.

One was astonished straightaway by the framed views of ocean and city, the rare luxury of a travertine balcony in the sky. But one was similarly surprised by just how accommodating the place was. Wheelchairs made the trek up and down walkways, from pavilion to garden to framed prospect, amenable to the aged, and my father was certainly game. And thus it was that I had my Getty-inspired exercise regimen prescribed for an afternoon.

It was not easy work, wheeling two hundred pounds and more of paternity up and down the ramps, and the inspirational uplift provided by the collection, most strikingly in the nineteenth century, alleviated the burden only slightly. It was the framed views of valley, city, and ocean that drew one on.

It was not until after I had left room 202 in the West Pavilion, a room so generally undistinguished that it went unmentioned in the official brochure, that things began, once again, to click. A generally forgettable nineteenth-century painting by a little-known Englishman had jolted me unexpectedly. Might it have been the subject? It was called "Mercy" and showed the young David ostentatiously sparing the life of a reclining King Saul. Specifically, the young hero orders his aide *not* to run the sleeping monarch through with a spear. I was familiar with Gide's treatment of the same motif, which I had attended to some years back in a book on anti-

Semitism. For Gide—but was it biblical too?—David was interested above all in demonstrating to Saul that he had no designs on his life. So after coming upon Saul asleep in a cave, he clips off a piece of the king's robe in order to be able to show, later on, that had he wanted to kill Saul, nothing would have prevented him, the snatch of cloth from the kingly robe demonstrating clearly that David had not lacked an opportunity.

The painting, by way of the recollection out of Gide, bore the strangest of kinetic fruit a mere five minutes later. As I strained to wheel my father up the travertine—no, as I struggled to prevent him from rolling too quickly *down* the travertine and into the panorama—it occurred to me that here was my long-awaited chance to release him, that is, *not* to release him into the multihued glory of a southern California sunset. David, that is, was I. Or rather would be, if I could imagine my father, then eighty-six, reacting to my phantasmagoria with anything other than a mixture of confusion and annoyance.

So I filed the fantasy in some pocket of my narcissism and proceeded to reward myself for this newfound combination of erudition and virtue by accepting my father's generosity in hosting my wife and me in a delectable dinner overlooking the very sunset from which my aching wrists had spared him.

Erudition? There remained my embarrassing ignorance of the painter who had so effectively scripted my trip to the Getty. It was, in fact, a month or two later, in Boston, that I decided to remedy that ignorance. The words "Saul David Getty," typed into the oblong box provided by my search engine, quickly revealed that the painter who had so flattered my narcissism, so inured it to the claims of Oedipus—but what was psychoanalysis, I would occasionally ask my class, if not the conviction that we are, all of us, condemned to act out both myths simultaneously?—the painter was one Richard Dadd.

And then came the revelation. The painting had been executed in the Criminal Lunatic Department of Bethlem Royal Hospital, the asylum to which Dadd had been consigned in 1844, after murdering his father in a delusional fit. The painting, it was commonly agreed, was a brilliantly executed denial of a parricide that had actually taken place. And it was a painting I had all but declared my own. I may have been right to claim that Dadd's David was I, but if so, I had identified with delusion itself. And whether he had known it or not, the retired merchant from Eighty-fourth Street would have found in my apparent defense, against an accusation he had no doubt long since forgotten, the clinching argument for the prosecution.

*

I began these notes three days ago, on a Boston–Los Angeles flight, with a childhood recollection of Kandahar in New York. I write now on the return flight after tending to my father, who lies semicomatose even as I write, apparently dying, in a cheerful Encino hospital, of pneumonia. Barely had I arrived in his Encino apartment than I was summoned to the intensive care unit by a supervising nurse intent on persuading—no, badgering—me into giving my father up. Time to let him go, I thought, but the thought immediately translated into a strain in my wrists, and I held on—as at the Getty. Richard Dadd may have called his painting "Mercy," but its legend of a death forestalled was palpably a relic of an age before mercy killings.

I had fortunately read my father's "living will" on the plane to California and was certain that it would take more than an impatient nurse—the stipulation was two doctors—for me to envisage shutting down the ample congeries of tubes and machines that appeared to be sustaining him.

Or was it that oldest of counsels, imparted to me by him in my childhood: "If anything happens to me, head first to the safety deposit box"? Was *I* the one who had gotten things precisely wrong this time? Might I have been keeping him alive—to the point of what the nurse regarded as torture—for the sake of the money? And all out of strict fidelity to his oldest teaching.

Fortunately, he weathered the crisis of that first night in Encino. Moreover, a newly administered antibiotic would need time to work. Early the next morning, I called David, a childhood friend who was none other than the son of my father's second wife. He is a prominent epidemiologist and was generously riding herd over the crew of doctors attending to my father. He confirmed me in my resisting the hectoring nurse, reminding me that in California's youth culture the presumption that only the young have a right to live had issued in some particularly nasty medical habits.

Richard Dadd's painting again loomed before me. Supine Saul, with his bin Laden beard and turban, was still my father, whose name—have I said so?—is in fact Saul. But Dadd's David had modulated into my friend David, instructing his robed aide to lay down his spear (or was it her syringe?) and spare Saul's life. I was out of the picture, as medicine frequently prefers it for the uninitiated, but the picture had only grown in hallucinatory accuracy.

Soon, I realize, my father too will be out of the picture. May that moment, when it comes—when? my plane lands in Boston in less than an hour and I dread the news—serve as a bond, both of us "out of the picture," as compelling as the one we knew a half century ago that afternoon at Kandahar in New York.

TEACHERS

7

Chiasmus

"Every existence," Paul Morand somewhere wrote, "is an anonymously sent letter."[1] Morand himself was happy to have figured out the provenance of the three postmarks (Paris, London, Venice) authenticating the letter his life had been, but his metaphor invites a more ambitious discovery: that of the author, if not the contents, of the missive programming one's existence. Lacan here finds himself curiously allied with Morand: it is the trajectory, the displacements of the inevitably "purloined" letter, rather than its contents or author, that align it with the fate of an individual. And yet who, of those who have bought into the epistolary metaphor, cannot at some point have entertained the well nigh theological dream of determining the date and author of the letter one's life will have been? Until recently, I was not among them. Lacan's fabled seminar on the Poe text, which I had translated in a state of protracted febrility I still dimly recall, had seemed a *nec plus ultra* beyond which I had no pretension of going.[2] Even Benjamin, in a short text I translated more recently under the title "Stamp Scams" (compressed from the German "Briefmarkenschwindel"), a kind of child's version of "The Work of Art in the Age of Mechanical Reproduction," was convinced that the future of the epistolary genre, or at least of its aesthetic pretensions, lay, beyond content, beyond the aura of (even the rarest of) postage stamps, in some future ornateness of the postmark per se.[3]

And then, several months ago, as a series of serendipitous finds allowed me to decipher the postmarks on the letter of my life as a (writing) reader, it suddenly dawned on me that the first of those marks—Cambridge, England, 1927, seventeen years before my birth—offered a decisive clue as to the author of my reading (and writing) days. These thoughts, then, on the path to his identification.

*

Boston 1983. I begin with the last of those postmarks—or cancellations—and shall work backward. Matters in this case begin at the Bibliothèque nationale in 1977 with my stumbling on what may be some of the most taboo texts of contemporary French letters: the series of violently antidemocratic, anti-Semitic, and proterrorist articles contributed in the 1930s by Maurice Blanchot to the fascist monthly *Combat*. Blanchot had been a tutelary presence for much of my previous work. My debt to him had been amply recorded in my essay of 1974, "Orphée scripteur," which was well received in the Blanchotian milieu.[4] Moreover, one of the more intriguing aspects of his writing was the constant strain toward Judaic metaphor in his delineation of a crucial realm of textual dispersion. Here, then, in the transition from the prewar anti-Semitic journalism to the postwar philo-Semitic meditation on "literary space" lay an enigma I set myself to pondering. The result was "Of Literature and Terror: Blanchot at *Combat*," which became the first chapter of my *Legacies: Of Anti-Semitism in France*.[5] But it is in the prehistory of that publication that the surprise imprint of my fourth postmark, a cancellation stunning in the breadth of what it appeared to cancel, inheres.

The essay situated Blanchot's former anti-Semitism against the strange backdrop of France's pre–World War II tradition of anti-Jewish thought and its precipitous liquidation once Hitler in effect made of anti-Semitism an untenable option for the vast majority of French intellectuals. My claim was that the—Möbius strip of a—context against which the Blanchot enigma might best be situated was the lineage moving from Edouard Drumont to Georges Bernanos to Maurice Clavel. Drumont, in *La France juive* (1886), wrote a thousand pages intent on promoting left-wing anticapitalist anti-Semitism as *the* political philosophy of modern times. It was one of the two best-selling works in France in the latter half of the nineteenth century.[6] The Catholic novelist and polemicist Bernanos, in his influential *La Grande peur des bien-pensants* (1931), wrote a lengthy biography in praise of Drumont. By the end of the decade,

Bernanos's politics had taken a militantly antifascist (i.e., anti-Francoist) turn, but he was careful to maintain that even then he had not broken with the values of his beloved "master," Drumont. Finally, there came in the 1970s the Catholic *gauchiste* patron of the resolutely *philo-Semitic* "new philosophers," Maurice Clavel. For Clavel was careful to maintain that *his* "master" remained Bernanos, and even the unassimilable Bernanos of *La Grande peur*. From Drumont to Bernanos to Clavel, in brief, there was no break but a paradoxical twist bringing a fundamentally anti-Semitic configuration into alignment with a later philo-Semitic one. Such, in summary, was the perverse progress against which I assayed the enigma I had located in Blanchot.

The essay first appeared in 1980 in a special issue of *Modern Language Notes* dedicated to the 1930s in France.[7] Meanwhile Philippe Sollers, who had heard a version of the paper (in improvised French) at Columbia University, confirmed that he was eager to publish a French translation (which he would commisssion) in *Tel Quel.* When the translation finally did appear, in 1982, it was riddled with misrenderings in French, but nonetheless provoked considerable interest pro and con in the French press—all without my knowledge. It was not until a number of months later that I saw the botched translation and the two principal articles devoted to my own. The first, in *Le Matin*, hailed a major and barely believable revelation and declared it particularly significant that France would have had to wait for an American to reveal matters of such import about French intellectual life.[8] The second, in *La Quinzaine littéraire*, simply denied the premise of my piece, refused to credit the existence of any anti-Semitic writings in Blanchot's past, and more or less implied that only a foreigner would stoop to such slander against the great French monument.[9] Given the opportunity for ridicule opened up by some of the more ludicrous errors in the translation of my essay, I confess that I was relieved to see the attack focusing on the article's premise, and dashed off a letter to Maurice Nadeau, the editor of *La Quinzaine*, in which I dissociated myself from the translation, responded nonetheless to the denial by quoting at some length two particularly hair-raising passages of anti-Jewish polemic by Blanchot in the 1930s, took the liberty of connecting the refusal to acknowledge the existence of such passages with the manifestly xenophobic tenor of the attack, and had the pleasure of ending my letter by paraphrasing a well-known Bernanos title: "Français, si vous saviez . . . l'anglais par exemple."

When a month passed without word from the *Quinzaine,* I called up Nadeau and was told to my surprise that he had received the letter but could not publish the two passages I had quoted because they were just too violent; Blanchot was now too old—and a friend of the house to boot. I reminded him that I had been attacked in his journal for claiming that such passages existed, specified that their existence could (and should) be carefully circumscribed in the *Quinzaine* by documenting Blanchot's activities during the war in the margins of the Resistance, but insisted that he publish my letter as written.[10] At which point he pleaded a faulty (overseas) connection and I hung up—in astonishment. When Sollers discovered the existence of my letter, he was all too happy to publish it in the first issue of *L'Infini* (as the newly relocated *Tel Quel* has since been called).[11] What measure of Parisian resentment dictated the relish with which Nadeau's refusal to publish the letter was announced in *L'Infini* is, of course, open to speculation.

Now, at the time all this was transpiring, my teaching in Boston brought me to review comments I had made years earlier in a preface to Jean Laplanche's *Life and Death in Psychoanalysis.*[12] In that piece, I saw myself (ten years after the fact) brandishing the thousand presumably unreadable pages of Lacan's *Ecrits* and telling my American readership that what was remarkable about the French reading of Freud was not simply that it was an alternative interpretation, different from the going American one, but that what it mediated was nothing so much as an elaborate theory of the inevitability of the error entailed by the American reading. Of a sudden, it dawned on me that the very same scenario was being reenacted—but in reverse—ten years later in the controversy surrounding my essay on Blanchot. For I saw myself this time—or so the *Quinzaine* would have it—in the position of the American who could not but be wrong. The seal provided by the twin motifs of the "inevitability of American error" and the thousand-page "unreadable" Gallic text (Drumont, Lacan) was unmistakable. As in Lacan's "Seminar on 'The Purloined Letter,'" an identical structure was being mobilized, but with a change of sign. As though the discursive dilemma into which I had been written in the recent polemic had always already been scripted in the somewhat triumphant heralding of the accomplishments of French thought found in my earlier essays.

Much of my subsequent work, in particular the essays collected in *Genealogies of the Text,* may be read as an effort to dwell within that unsettling insight in the hope of seeing where it might lead. It was as though the new imperative lay in returning to my earlier analyses of a variety of authors as though they had been *at best* virtuoso renditions of the treble part of works for which I could now supply a rather rich, though sinister, bass.[13] But my concern here is less prospective than archeological. From that perspective, the chiasmus pitting the Blanchot episode against the Laplanche preface, one Franco-American interaction against another, in fact harks back to the culminating figure, a chiasmus, in Laplanche's reading of Freud in his volume of 1970. One postmark or "cancellation" may cancel out another, but each, to the extent that it is a chiasmus, is above all intent on canceling *itself.* As the case of the penultimate of our postmarks, figured by the concluding figure of Laplanche's book, will make clear.

*

Paris 1970. *Vie et mort en psychanalyse* remains the most remarkable exercise in reading I know. That it is a reading of a would-be scientific text rather than a work of literature is an inconvenience for professionals of reading, but only because of the small-mindedness of academic bureaucracies. But what is it that leads me to endow that work with such centrality? Consider the terms of Laplanche's reading. For each of a series of crucial terms in Freud, Laplanche succeeds in demonstrating that there are two incompatible meanings at work. Moreover, if one strings together one set of meanings (for the sequence of terms), one arrives at an entirely coherent interpretative scheme, which we may dub Scheme A. And if one strings together the second member of each conceptual doublet, a second interpretative scheme, coherent in its own terms, may be generated: call it Scheme B. Laplanche thus is able to constitute the entirety of Freud's oeuvre as a polemical field in which two interpretative schemes— A and B—do battle to invest a single terminological apparatus.

But the situation is more intricate still. For Laplanche shows (without quite stating as much explicitly) that whereas Scheme A (corresponding, say, to American ego psychology) affirms its coherence in utter innocence—or ignorance—of Scheme B, what Scheme B (corresponding, say, to Lacan's structural recasting of Freud) mediates, as suggested above, is nothing so much as a theory of the inevitability of the error constituted by the "A" reading of Freud. Put in other terms: if the irreducibility of the fact of repression is the central discovery of psychoanalysis, and if that discovery is itself under constant threat of repression, then Scheme A (according to Scheme B) would be the precise form taken by the repression of all that had been wrested from the unconscious by way of Scheme B. The more Dupin, in Lacan's heuristic reading of Poe, held on to the purloined letter, the more he seemed neurotically possessed by it. Just so, the more Freud attempted to consolidate his theory of "unconscious sexuality," the more that term proved vulnerable to the—fundamentally narcissistic, and thus repressive—prerogatives of the agency of "consolidation" or libidinal unification in the psyche, the "ego." "Unconscious sexuality," the very life of Freud's unconscious, is thus metamorphosed into "Eros," the unifying or "binding" principle of the unconscious's diacritical *other*, the ego. But simultaneously, in Freud's metapsychology, the original *other* of the unconscious, the ego (or what Freud calls "ego instincts") is metamorphosed into something beyond (or other than) Eros and its reassuring (because narcissistic) "pleasure principle": a "death instinct," whose structure is at bottom indistinguishable from that of the unconscious itself. The whole process mediates what Laplanche regards as an unwitting reaffirmation of the priority of the unconscious at a time when the very terms that had originally served to articulate that dimension (or discovery) had in large measure been reclaimed, reinvested by the "binding" agency of the narcissistic ego. It is a process enabled in part by Freud's misexploitation of a distinction—between "free" and "bound" energy—borrowed from Helmholtz: Helmholtz's "free" or "freely usable" energy became Freud's free-flowing or "unbound" unconscious affect, even as the physicist's "bound" or "unavailable" energy became the "bound" and thus stable and disposable affect of Freud's ego. But the key element to note is that the entire process is an unwitting crisscross or chiasmus underpinning the entirety of Freud's metapsychology, as Laplanche's concluding diagram indicates (see Figure 1).

Between Boston 1983 and Paris 1970, my two most recent "postmarks" or "cancellations," a chiasmus had been enacted. But I have little doubt that the crisscross was at some level dictated or inspired by the chiasmus informing what I had come to regard as *the* exemplary act of reading, Laplanche's interpretation of Freud. The intricate disappointment of Boston 1983 had in some measure canceled out the heady enthusiasm of Paris 1970, but it was in large measure because the subject of that earlier enthusiasm had been a delineation of the perverse rigor with which an exemplary *oeuvre* had been seen to be hell-bent on canceling itself.

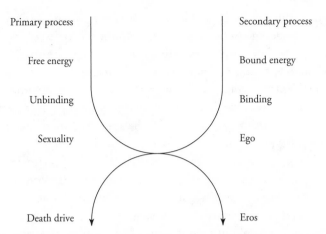

Primary process

Free energy

Unbinding

Sexuality

Death drive

Secondary process

Bound energy

Binding

Ego

Eros

FIGURE I. The hidden structure of Freud's metapsychology. From Jean Laplanche, *Life and Death in Psychoanalysis* (Baltimore: Johns Hopkins University Press, 1976), p. 124.

*

Aix-en-Provence 1966. If I was in a position to register the full import of Laplanche's reading of Freud (behind which, of course, lay Lacan's own reevaluations), it was because I had read close to the complete works of Freud at the Yale Medical School while a graduate student in French literature in the late 1960s in New Haven. But my reason for undertaking the Freud project in those years grew out of the year—1965–66—I spent as a Fulbright Fellow in Aix-en-Provence. For it was there that I had a readerly revelation, the third of the "postmarks" to which I shall attend, though the second chronologically, fully as determinative as the one bearing the imprint "Paris 1970." Indeed, it may be suggested in anticipation that if "Boston 1983" appeared to repeat, even as it reversed, "Paris 1970," the latter, I have but recently come to realize, functioned as a repetition of "Aix-en-Provence 1966."

It was during that Fulbright year that, as part of a miniscule cohort of foreign students, I attended the public lectures of Charles Mauron, serving, during that last year of his life, in a state of total blindness, as an adjunct professor at the Faculté des lettres of Aix-en-Provence. Mauron, in the 1930s and 1940s, had been a prominent figure of the heroic age of Mallarmé exegesis, deciphering the extraordinarily oblique and formally polished poems whose importance seems never to have been in doubt, but whose meaning emphatically was. Mauron succeeded in glossing the poems but was above all alive to a dimension he called, borrowing a phrase from Mallarmé, a *miroitement en-dessous*: a shimmering below the surface. For he had noted a whole series of images, indeed a structured conflict, whose logic was invisible in any individual poem but perceptible solely in the interplay between poems. Plainly, the "personal myth," as he would later call it, was, in its invisibility to a reading of individual poems, unintended. Yet what was one to make of it? An answer of sorts was provided with the posthumous publication of a narrative dating from Mallarmé's adolescence.[14] For not only was it an all but explicit version of the "myth" Mauron could perceive only in the interstices (or resonances) between the poems of the poet's maturity, but it was dated shortly after the traumatic death of the poet's sister. With the figure in Mallarmé's carpet so tied to a personal trauma, Mauron found himself backing into a psychoanalytic interpretation, almost in spite of himself. The impressive result was *Introduction à la psychanalyse de Mallarmé*.[15]

More pertinent in the current context was Mauron's effort to see whether the limit case of Mallarmé might in some way be generalized. Might it not be possible to generate possibilities as radical as those he had stumbled upon in his exegesis of Mallarmé in readings of other authors, to free up, as it were, a Mallarméan stratum in still other texts? (But was not my later effort, for better or worse, to export all that seemed at stake in my Blanchot episode—of Boston 1983—to other regions of French literature a form of fidelity to this gesture of Mauron's?) On his way to an answer, Mauron adopted as a heuristic model Francis Galton's technique of superimposing the negatives of photographs of members of the same family. Individual features were blurred out as a bizarre composite portrait emerged. Might one not perform similarly strange exploits with, say, the texts of a single author? The superimposition of texts, a far dicier proposition than comparison, would generate the unintended myth, textual counterpart to Galton's composite portrait, and the myth's evolution could then be analyzed in psychoanalytic terms. Only in a final stage would the author's life be invoked as a form of control: for the very myth that played itself out subliminally in the evolution of an author's work was presumably acted out simultaneously, in however indirect a manner, in his life.

It was in 1957 that Mauron published his first large-scale exercise in superimposition, a volume on the "work and life of Racine."[16] The results were fully as astonishing to me in "Aix 1966" as my reading of Laplanche in "Paris 1970," the following postmark on the letter of my reading life, would be. Stack up the major tragedies of Racine and a hidden drama may be seen to be playing itself out: A male attempts to free himself from the clutches of an aggressive and somewhat virile female, who reproaches him for his ingratitude. He in turn wants no more than to flee and share the misfortune of a melancholic younger woman, his captive. When the male's project finally succeeds, a new character, a father, appears, and under the pressure exerted by his presence, the male is forced to retreat from his new-found happiness back into the psychic orbit of the reproachful and aggressive woman, who all but swallows him up. Phèdre, that is, succeeds in dragging Hippolyte to his death along with her, even if Racine ends up modifying Euripides' plot in fundamental ways in order to assure that outcome. At which point Racine abandons the theatre and reconciles with Port-Royal, the reproachful Jansenist matriarchy of his orphan years. Phèdre, in sum, is to Hippolyte as Port-Royal is to Racine and as a somewhat exhibitionistic and masochistic Aricie is to the theatre itself. Life and work enact and are subtended by a single myth.[17]

There was, it seemed to me, a weak moment in Mauron's analysis: the tethering of what were frequently spectacular textual superimpositions to ready-made (Oedipal) schemata out of Freud. Now, it happened (such would be the upshot of "Paris 1970") that around Lacan, in Paris, Freud was being destabilized, read in exactly the same spirit as Racine had been read by Mauron in Aix. So the critical task might lie in opening up Mauron's psychoanalytic readings of texts to the new Freudian dispensation—say, the lesson of Laplanche—coming out of Paris. And indeed, much of my early work—on Baudelaire and on Valéry, among others—might be read in precisely those terms.

And yet it was sufficient to observe the precise contours of the Racinian superscore, modulating from play to play, to realize that what was transpiring between Mauron's Racine and Laplanche's Freud was more on the order of a repetition than a corrective. Consider the Racine *schéma* as it appears in *L'Inconscient dans l'oeuvre et la vie de Racine*, shown in Figure 2.

For our present purposes, we need not dwell at any length on the details of the plays. Two facts, however, should be mentioned. First was my sheer sense of elation at seeing the intricacy of the structure within

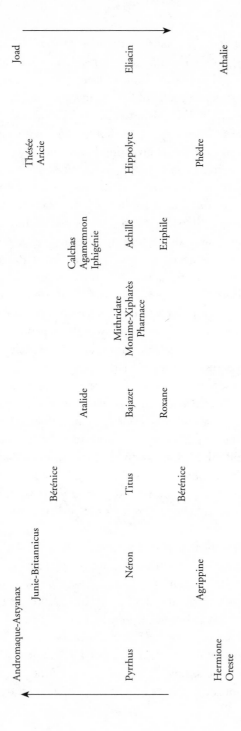

FIGURE 2. Racine's eight tragedies together reconstituted as a musical score. From Charles Mauron, *L'Inconscient dans l'oeuvre et la vie de Racine* (Gap: Edition Ophrys, 1957), p. 27.

which Mauron managed to choreograph the relations among the characters of eight separate tragedies. I have encountered an analogous experience of readerly joy only in Valéry's comments on his exposure to Mallarmé: "I undertook to reconstruct the constructor of such a work. It seemed to me that such a work must have been indefinitely reflected within a mental enclosure from which nothing was free to escape without having *dwelt* at length in a world of presentiments, harmonic arrangements, perfect figures and their corresponding forms; a world of anticipations in which everything made contact with everything else, and in which chance itself paused, oriented itself, and finally crystallized into a model."[18] But, of course, to the extent that Mauron approached Racine with the intent of freeing up what might be called a Mallarméan stratum in Racine, the Valéry/Mallarmé nexus seems oddly apposite. Emerging from my undergraduate years at Harvard into the sunlight of Mauron's analyses, I too had the feeling, as Valéry said of Mallarmé, that in a world where others were doing arithmetic, I had discovered algebra. (It was an experience, to be sure, that complicated my subsequent years as a graduate student at Yale.)

The second element worth underscoring is that it is enough to rotate Mauron's diagram ninety degrees for it to assume the shape of a chiasmus. The inverse relation between the arrows at the top and bottom of the page designates the changed direction of the principal aggression in the play: issuing from a reproachful "maternal" presence in the first half of Racine's *oeuvre* (*Andromaque, Britannicus, Bérénice, Bajazet*) and from a vengeful or castratory father in the second (*Mithridate, Iphigénie, Phèdre,* and finally *Athalie*). Moreover, the point of intersection of the two arrows, the crux of the chiasmus, lies in the return of a vengeful father (who keeps on "returning") once the quasi-incestuous union of *Mithridate* is effected.

So the unwitting underlying structure of Racine's theatre (*pace* Mauron) forms the same (chiastic) figure as that underpinning Freud's *Gesammelte Schriften* (as read by Laplanche). My efforts to revise and correct, as it were, many of Mauron's stunning superimpositions of literary texts by freeing them from the residually naive versions of Freud to which they had been tethered, and to do so by way of an extrapolation from Laplanche's readings of Freud, had over and again borne their fruit, but at some level, chiasmus for chiasmus, *both* readings, Mauron's *and* Laplanche's, were versions of each other. Paris 1970, in a deep sense, turned out for me to be more repetition than correction of Aix-en-Provence 1966.

*

I have mentioned that my enthusiasm for Mauron's readings had not entirely facilitated my life as a graduate student at Yale. For it had seemed to me that he was plainly functioning at an intellectual and critical level far beyond what was being dispensed in New Haven (or, for that matter, in the Cambridge I had known). My sense was that in Mauron I had encountered a thinker both surprising and convincing, a rare combination. For if the Harvard of my undergraduate years had been so much more convincing in its teaching than surprising that it courted the soporific, and if the Yale that followed was soon to be so much more surprising than convincing in *its* teaching that it at times approached the zany, Mauron, whom I had known between the two, seemed alone among the critics I then knew to have combined the two dimensions to a degree that might be regarded as *tonic*. And I was sufficiently cognizant of that fact to alienate some, both students and faculty, who were convinced that Yale represented a critical horizon beyond which it would be folly to pretend to look.

In that somewhat uncomfortable situation, however, I was buoyed by a knowledge, at the time only glimpsed, that long before I was born the leading figures of another generation, in another country, had experienced the very same elation at the genius of the Provençal critic. For Charles Mauron was, in a word, Bloomsbury's favorite Frenchman. It was Roger Fry who first met up with Mauron, in 1919, and he remained under the spell for the rest of his life. After bringing Mauron to London for a visit, he would write Vanessa Bell: "He is a delightful creature & I wish you had been there. He has such extraordinary sensibility of all kinds which makes it a delight to show him things. Perhaps I enjoy him more than anyone because in so many ways our reactions are exactly similar to music & literature as well as to painting."[19] Upon reading a Mauron essay on aesthetics, he commented: "I am in ecstasy before the style, the charm, the humour of it. Here we are once more in the 18th century, when people knew how to appreciate intellectual delight. And how different its style is from all the weighty, the heavy accent, the serious feeling to say nothing of the willed obscurity of our thinkers. . . . Really I can't tell you how exquisite I find it."[20] Fry's bedazzlement by the Frenchman, who was sinking into blindness throughout their friendship, is amply chronicled in Virginia Woolf's biography of Fry. The imperative of Fry's later years is evoked by Woolf as follows: "Theories must be discussed, preferably with someone like Charles Mauron, who could demolish them."[21] Or in Fry's own words (as cited by Woolf): "Charles Mauron is so terribly good at analysis that it sometimes seems impossible to make any positive construction that will resist his acids. . . . I suppose you feel like that with me, that I will go on analysing when you want to take a certain whole and look without pulling it apart. Only as I never feel clear in my mind without having analysed as far as possible, I have to applaud his destruction even of my cherished ideas."[22] But Fry's estimation of Mauron was widespread in Bloomsbury. Years later, Quentin Bell would write: "I have in my time met a good many people who could be classed as intellectuals. People who when they have been offered an idea will set upon it joyously and pursue it with unflagging enthusiasm, but none who had such an appetite and stamina for the chase as Charles Mauron. He talked endlessly, brilliantly and continuously with an erudition which he never took for granted. He was sometimes comic, often profound and never boring."[23] Virginia Woolf herself was swept up in the enthusiasm. Of Mauron's introduction to a Mallarmé project brought out jointly with Fry and Julian Bell, she would write in November 1936: "I think Mauron's introduction one of the best pieces of criticism I've read this blue moon. He's so clear, so subtle and so witty all in one."[24] On April 28, 1940, she would write him from Monk's House: "Partly because you are French—and also because you are so fine a thinker—I feel I could learn more from you about writing than from any English critic."[25] But perhaps her ultimate tribute to Mauron is the mention he receives at the end of her heart-rending suicide note to Leonard Woolf, the note that begins, "I want to tell you that you have given me complete happiness," and ends with a postscript: "You will find Roger's letters to the Maurons in the writing table drawer in the Lodge. Will you destroy my papers?"[26] That last mention—the name and the texts that will alone be spared destruction—reads almost like a legacy.

At which point the reader is granted a sense, by Bloomsbury *interposé*, of the enthusiasm I was not alone, but perhaps at that late date one of the relatively few, to feel for the then completely blind Mauron. Indeed, as one perceives the apparent contagion affecting reactions to the Frenchman, one can even intuit the resentments or incredulity of those who were exposed to such unmitigated rapture. The circumstance maintained already in Bloomsbury. Edward Playfair, Julian Bell's friend, before join-ing the cult, admitted an understandable initial prejudice against Mauron and his wife.[27] As he wrote Bell, "I was prepared—you know how one is in those circumstances—after having heard so much praise of them, to be rather disappointed."[28] Such was a bit the resentment I encountered (or provoked through my own enthusiasm) thirty years later in New Haven.

It is not a psychological or sentimental ambiance that I am chart-ing here, however, but the repetitive persistence of the most diaphanous of figures. Which brings us to a final habitué of Bloomsbury and a final legacy, that of E. M. Forster. Shortly after Fry had commissioned Mauron to translate *A Passage to India* (other Forster novels would follow) in the 1920s, Forster and Mauron struck up a remarkably intense friendship. In *Two Cheers for Democracy*, Mauron, who was by then totally blind, is called—a painful irony—"the friend who, after Roger Fry, has helped me with pictures most."[29] Indeed, the Forster-Mauron friendship seems to have flourished under the sign of tragedy. In his essay "Ferney," For-ster describes the visit the two of them made in June 1939, on the brink of a world conflagration, to that temple of sanity, Voltaire's retreat near the Franco-Swiss border. Two intellectuals, the "last of [their] sinewy tribe," get a "last peep at one of the symbols of European civilisation."[30] Two "cultivated monkeys," that is, will soon be made to depart for their "re-spective cages"—France, England—to be "closed and locked" not long after they enter them. The tragedy of World War II was, for Forster, not least that of the loss of his "beloved and lost Charles Mauron," as he wrote to Forrest Reid in September 1940, shortly after the beginning of the Oc-cupation.[31] He would seek consolation by transcribing passages from Mauron's letters into his *Commonplace Book*. And his thoughts as he did so, as reported in a letter of March 1943 to John Hampson, are remark-able: "I am all ruffled by Churchill's hideous heartless shifty speech, too much of which has come through our wireless, and must comfort myself by a line to you before I go to bed, I was a bit wrought up anyhow, as I have been transcribing and destroying Charles Mauron's letters for most of the day, and realising I shall never see him again, and then I have to en-dure this dentured dotard telling me I live in a glorious age."[32] Mauron vs. Churchill.[33] Has Forster ever come closer to identifying the friend rather than whom he would prefer to betray his country, in the most famous line of *Two Cheers for Democracy*?

Charles Mauron was the dedicatee of Forster's *Aspects of the Novel* in 1927. And of all the discussions in that memorable book, originally the Clark Lectures at Trinity College, Cambridge, of that same year, the one that has attracted the most attention, not all of it positive, is that of Henry James's *The Ambassadors*. If Forster was indeed the "only living novelist" capable of eliciting from Lionel Trilling, in 1943, with each re-reading, the "sensation of having learned something," one is surprised to find the critic so little surprised at his sense of the vapidity of Forster's discussion of James: "Most disappointing of all from Forster is the treatment of Henry James, beginning with its stale joke about James's snobbery and his horror of being compared with the shopkeeping Richardson. . . . Obviously, not only energy has failed here, but with it intelligence."[34]

The discussion of *The Ambassadors* occurs memorably in the chapter of *Aspects* on "Pattern and Rhythm," where it emerges that the novelistic pattern par excellence is what Forster calls the "hourglass" and the novel that best instantiates it *The Ambassadors*. Forster recounts the plot with some gusto: Middle-aged Lambert Strether is commissioned by the Massachusetts matron to whom he is engaged to go to Paris and rescue her son Chad, "who has gone to the bad in that appropriate city."[35] When he discovers a Chad not ruined but refined, indeed "redeemed" by Paris, he switches sides, "remains in Paris not to fight it but to fight for it."[36] Thus does an ambassador betray or go native. Whereupon a new slew of ambassadors arrives from Massachusetts. Strether fights them down, only to surmise that Chad himself is "played out." "Is not Chad's Paris after all just a place for a spree?"[37] When Chad himself opts to return to the vulgar normalcy of Woolett, Massachusetts, "the pattern of the hourglass is complete": he and Strether have changed places.[38] The elegance of the chiasmus is duly saluted, but quickly gives way to a series of reservations. The choreography of the characters in their alignment with the hourglass or chiasmus exacts too high a price, we are told, for the vitality of a fictional character cannot be made to conform to so abstract a pattern. James stands accused of staging a "drastic curtailment," a "maiming," indeed a "castrating" on behalf of pattern. "Beauty has arrived, but in too tyrannous a guise. In plays—the plays of Racine, for instance—she may be justified because beauty can be a great empress on the stage, and reconcile us to the loss of the men we knew. But in the novel, her tyranny as it grows powerful grows petty."[39] Consider, then, that in *The Ambassadors*, the novel, as Philip Fisher has memorably put it, in which an entire academic generation "saw its own love of criticism, observation, nuance, disappointment, myth, and defeat," Forster manages to isolate the three key elements of chiasmus (the "hourglass"), castration, and Racine.[40] But the Mauron volume of 1957, the stuff of my revelation of "Aix 1966," it will be recalled, was a reading of Racine structured by a chiasmus at whose crux or point of reversal lay the return of a punitive, indeed castrating, father (Mithridate). It would appear that Forster's letter of "Cambridge 1927," the dedication of *Aspects of the Novel*, was (unwittingly?) received as the (unwitting) structure or chiasmus of "Aix 1966."

It would be tempting to pursue the regress beyond Cambridge 1927. Trilling, after all—and with more precision Frederick Crews—has insisted that Forster's first published novel, *Where Angels Fear to Tread*, may be usefully regarded as a reworking of the plot of *The Ambassadors*.[41] Forster's Philip leaves puritanical, philistine Sawston for Italy much as James's Strether had left puritanical, philistine Woolett for France. Each novel ends up recounting the drama of what Forster called the "undeveloped heart."[42] And on the penultimate page, where Forster would drive home a fundamental incompatibility between his two cultures, a telling mythological reference surfaces. Philip Herriton tries to imagine the mating of the quintessentially English Miss Abbott with the wild Italian she has fallen in love with: "He smiled bitterly at the thought of them together. Here was the cruel antique malice of the gods, such as they once sent forth against Pasiphae."[43] Pasiphae, enamored of the bull, and the mother of Phaedra . . . Racine, with *The Ambassadors*, again.[44]

If I stop the regress here, however, it is because this last (or chronologically first) chiasmus, Forster's hourglass, meshes so curiously with the first (or chronologically last) we discussed. A review of our four figures, the four postmarks on the letter of my life as a reader, will make this clear. "Cambridge 1927," with its key elements of hourglass (or chiasmus), castration, and Racine, metamorphosed, in the fullness of time, into Mauron's volume on Racine and the readerly revelation it brought me during my Fulbright year working with Mauron in "Aix 1966." But the chiasmus underpinning the structure of the entirety of Racine's *oeuvre* (in Mauron's Freudian reading) turned out to be an anticipation of a second crux in my readerly experience: the chiasmus underlying the entirety of Freud's metapsychology (and without which that metapsychology would remain opaque) in Laplanche's reading of "Paris 1970." Finally, "Boston 1983": at the heart of the Blanchot episode, two key elements present in my preface to Laplanche—the thousand-page, presumably unreadable French monument (Lacan's *Ecrits*, Drumont's *La France juive*); the theory of the "inevitability" of American error (American ego psychology *pace* Laplanche; my take on Blanchot *pace La Quinzaine littéraire*)—resurfaced, but in devastating reverse. "The thread," as Henry James once wrote to the Duchess of Sutherland about *The Ambassadors*, "is really stretched quite scientifically tight."[45] But the link with the James novel is deeper. For *The Ambassadors* is, among other things, the story of a return to America from a Paris it was impossible to love "enough without liking it too much."[46] I realize, in retrospect, that the episode of Boston 1983—Nadeau's refusal to print my letter, but my own sense of having somehow subliminally scripted the entire sequence—was the initiation of a return of sorts to America, born of a sense that the only way to love France might well be to love her too much. (The postmark "Boston 1983," I have suggested, was in every sense a cancellation.) My first book, *A Structural Study of Autobiography*, made its way into the heady waters of Lévi-Straussian structuralism more than a quarter of a century ago.[47] My most recent, *Emigré New York: French Intellectuals in Wartime Manhattan, 1940–1944*, ends with a chapter about Lévi-Strauss during his New York exile.[48] To the extent that the book manages to include my city and year of birth in its title, it is, I suspect, my most personal book, a return trip of sorts, but to say as much risks obscuring the import of these pages, the discovery that it was the unwitting repetition of a postmark—Cambridge 1927, Aix 1966, Paris 1970, Boston 1983—on a letter sent considerably before my birth, from a city I've visited only twice—that would seem to have oriented the apparent progress to wherever it is that I now, as the locution has it, am *at*.[49]

8

Derrida

We had quarreled some years back, so I was no longer in the loop. Still, I had known of Derrida's illness for about a year and was not altogether surprised to see the announcement of his death in the *Times*. Indeed, the placement of the obituary on the first page struck me as altogether appropriate, a kind of vindication of the intellectual labors and enthusiasms of the generation, my own, which had discovered his work in the age prior to its academic respectability. There was, after all, a time, the early seventies, when the urgent task in American academia seemed to be to bring Derrida, and the whole Franco-German nexus that was to form the core of what would soon be misnamed "literary theory," into English. The term "deconstruction," of course, is now omnipresent in the culture. (Auden's line, on the death of Freud, about "a whole climate of feeling" comes to mind.) And for years I had found myself subliminally noting deconstructive touches on the op-ed page of one prominent newspaper or another, trying to imagine in which elite university an author might have been exposed to Derrida's thought and picked up, say, a particular penchant for chiasmus which had worked its way from a long since forgotten course on literature to his or her present writing. I was convinced that one could no more *not* be marked by an encounter with his thought than I had been.

I was wrong, of course. The derisory, almost muckraking tone of the *Times* obituary felt like an ambush. The insistence that Derrida had never succeeded in coming up with anything less "murky" as a characterization of deconstruction than its own impossibility showed, above all, deep hostility to the entire effort. Surely one might have served up, as a guide to the uninitiated, say, Valéry's quip—deconstruction encapsulated on one foot, as the Talmudists might have said—that philosophy was a literary genre among others, and the comedy (or tragedy) of philosophy was that philosophers were the last ones to realize it. That (and numerous other luminous one-liners) might have been found throughout the early Derrida, but one would, to be sure, have to have *wanted* to find them. It was, finally, the failure to reveal any inkling of a new style of readerly complexity, the new obliqueness of coherence with which Derrida electrified much of a generation of literary scholars, that was most disappointing. As though at a certain level of obliqueness the screen went blank. The obituary, inevitably, latched on to the de Man affair, surely one of deconstruction's sorrier moments and one that played a role in the falling out I referred to at the beginning of these remarks. (I shall return to it.) But the net effect conveyed by our paper of record—that of a confused mind with a soft spot for anti-Semites—was so incompatible with the first-page placement of the article, unless it were intended less as an obituary than as a report on a widespread pathology, that any reader should immediately have been puzzled.

From my own perspective, I almost felt that what was needed was a contemporary rewrite of Péguy's *Notre jeunesse*, the legendary retrospective defense by the early Dreyfusard of the cause that had mobilized his own generation (and given currency to the word "intellectual"), even if that cause had eventually degenerated (as causes tend to) from what the author called *mystique* to *politique*. In the current context, I can perhaps contribute a few notes toward such a project, specifically concerning two episodes that marked turning points in my own engagement in (and withdrawal from) the "loop." What they have in common is an experience of shock at an unexpected blindness to the allures of deconstruction, allures one might feel obliged, on one ground or another, to resist but which one could not, or so I felt, fail to acknowledge. Whence the shock. It is precisely the shock experienced by many a reader of the recent obituary, which is what leads me to believe that its very anticipation in these two early episodes may have interest beyond the personal experiences they came to unsettle.

During the academic year 1974–75, at about the time the twin towers of *Glas* (but also of New York) were reaching completion, I was a visiting assistant professor in Berkeley, stunned by the cloudlessness of the San

Francisco fall and convinced, as I recall writing to Derrida, that the critique of visible *form* (to the benefit of invisible *force*) would not carry ultimate conviction until one *saw* how good things could look against that cloudless sky. (Michel Foucault, who was also visiting Berkeley for the first time that same year, had his own reasons for being besotted with the Northern California weather.) I was, at the time, enthralled with Derrida's project. If I have since come to think of his work as a series of more or less brilliant footnotes to Mallarmé, at the time I was not far from thinking of his grippingly oblique texts as those of a contemporary Mallarmé. (In retrospect, the judgment has a certain aptness: deconstruction marked the end of a hundred-year cycle during which thinking adventurously for much of the West meant thinking—or imagining—along with one French vanguard or another: Symbolism, Surrealism, Existentialism, Structuralism, Deconstruction . . . At the beginning of the sequence, Mallarmé; at the end, Derrida.) My mission, in sum, was to bring the good news, most immediately from Baltimore, deconstruction's original port of call, where I had just spent a year, to the West Coast.

Now, it happened that of those prepared to hear me out on the Berkeley campus the philosopher John Searle was among the most eager. Might I have made a proselyte? In my enthusiasm, I had failed to note that the charmingly contentious Searle had the philosophical temperament of a cop. The set of cross-purposes was not without its comic aspect. Whereas I thought I was conducting a conversion, he thought he had found a police informant who would feed him enough hard information to put a philosophical malefactor away for a good long time. Perhaps the encounter was doomed from the start. There was no way a school of thought centered on the exemplary speech act *my-word-is-my-bond* would look kindly on a philosopher then attending, in *Glas*, to the *erectile* potential (*sa-parole-bande*) of Hegel's text. Still, it was decided that a Derrida reading group would be formed at the home of Hubert Dreyfus, high in the Berkeley hills. In attendance, aside from Searle, Dreyfus, and myself, were Denis Hollier, who was also visiting Berkeley, and our chairman, Leo Bersani.

By the time of the second meeting, devoted, at Searle's request, to Derrida's essay on (Searle's former teacher) J. L. Austin, it was clear that those of us who knew French were being enlisted by Searle to help him get the goods on Derrida. The group disbanded amidst a general sentiment of failure: there would be no prosecution, and *certainly* no conversion. Still, the episode remained with me as an amusing case of what might have been. When I returned to Baltimore in 1975, several of us, with the still-vibrant dream of at last bringing the recent French intellectual effervescence home to English in a form worthy of it, found ourselves founding a journal, which the Johns Hopkins University Press decided to bring out as a serial called *Glyph*. I remember telling my fellow editor, Sam Weber, of the botched encounter with Searle, regretting that there was nothing to be salvaged from it. Sam was not convinced, or perhaps he felt that a failed encounter itself was an event important enough to merit entry into the annals of *Glyph*. I remember telling Sam that the only thing Searle was interested in was proclaiming Derrida's fraudulence, then thinking that if that were all he had to say, he certainly would not write it, since, among other things, he would have exhausted his message in a single page.

I called up Searle and invited him to comment on Derrida's text on Austin, which Sam and I would translate for the issue. To my surprise he accepted immediately, almost gleefully, and in short order we were publishing a text by Searle proclaiming the fraudulence of Derrida.[1] I imagine that the shock Derrida felt upon reading Searle's indictment of him must have been on the same order as the one many felt upon reading the obituaries in the *Times* and the *Economist*. Yet the piece exercised a certain fascination for him. After all, for Derrida, error, the structure of misprision, was a more interesting category than truth, and here, in Searle, was an error—the bad faith of Derrida—it would have been difficult, from his perspective, to surpass. The task was to write something that would *encompass* that error, make the case for its inevitability (even as these modest notes are an attempt to *situate*, in terms of a sequence of episodes, what seems to many of us to be the colossal wrongheadedness of the recent obituaries). The result was the lengthy and somewhat laborious "Limited Inc," in which the name Searle was contaminated by the French acronym SARL (*société à responsabilité limitée*) even as the self-possession and "punctuality" of would-be performers of "speech acts" found themselves undermined by the "iterability" of a phantom or parasitic illocutionary realm without which those acts would remain moot. Derrida's text was published in a subsequent issue of *Glyph*.[2]

It was about this time, I have been told, that word was beginning to spread throughout Yale that Europe's "greatest philosopher" happened to be not only in New Haven but, more improbably still, in the Yale French

Department. A decision was made to trot out Yale's new star before the larger Yale community, which inevitably meant before a number of local and not so local philanthropists. Unfortunately, the only unpublished text in English Derrida had was apparently the laboriously elaborated pun on the name of Searle. The result was a small (though seemingly interminable) disaster. There was no way the community at large would warm to Derrida's paradoxical and entirely counterintuitive argument. New Haven was prepared to have its intuitions refined, perhaps deepened, but not reversed. For that at bottom was the crux of America's allergy to Derrida's parapsychoanalytical project. I am told that well into the seemingly endless lecture, various Yale administrators convened in the lobby of the lecture hall to discuss damage control—and that Paul de Man had to be flown back in from Europe to put out the fire.

*

(I am suddenly reminded of Derrida's first lecture at Yale, at the very beginning of the seventies, at which I happened to be present. Once again anticipatory excitement surpassed comprehension. Speaking about Freud, Derrida, well into his lecture, cited, as was his wont since Grammatology, *a rather impressive paragraph by Jean Starobinski. The aim was to set up the most impressive of fall guys for the deconstructive assault. So impressive was Starobinski's rhetoric, however, so apparently unchallengeable his argument, and so late the hour, that the audience erupted into applause at what they took to be the conclusion of the lecture. I still recall Derrida's hapless shrug at the misdirected applause whose recipient he was. He agreed that his lecture was over. Derrida's first champion in New Haven, Jacques Ehrmann, who lay dying of kidney failure during that lecture, would have savored the moment. His favorite maxim: "Quand on voit un couillon dans l'erreur, on l'y laisse.")*

*

Let me turn now to a third episode, between the Searle encounter and the obituary, of apparent incomprehension of Derrida, one whose casualty was, in part, my own friendship with him. It relates to what has been called the "de Man affair." In 1978, as I have recounted in a previous chapter, I had been stunned to come across a number of rather compromising texts by Maurice Blanchot in the overtly fascist 1930s journal

Combat. The circumstance, which I recall sharing with Derrida, seemed to me an enigma worth pondering and to a number of others, in retrospect, a kind of dress rehearsal for the de Man incident. How indeed was one to understand the transition from the political writer exulting in acts of terrorism against Jews and Communists in the 1930s to the quietist philo-Semite (and patron saint of deconstruction) of the postwar years? The answer I came up with is less important in the current context than the fact that, because I was known to have been pondering such questions, *Newsweek* decided to interview me about the somewhat congruent case of Paul de Man.

Not long before the de Man incident erupted, I found myself giving (along with Barbara Johnson) one of two keynote addresses at a conference in Pennsylvania perversely dedicated to the theme of the "politics of literary adulation." I was sufficiently taken with the high-masochistic tenor of deconstruction, and perhaps sufficiently annoyed by the spectacle of those who were now climbing onto the deconstructive bandwagon in what had just recently become the age of its academic respectability, to want to go after the Derrida with whom I had identified at a time of greater risk. I might have called the piece "Has Success Spoiled JD?" but chose instead "Writing and Deference."[3] Derrida understandably never forgave me for choosing a title that could not even be mentioned without *les rieurs*, as Molière might have said, being on my side.

My theme was that if one wanted to gauge the waning of the intellectual energy of deconstruction, one would do well to consider Derrida's recent book *Parages*, a volume dedicated to Blanchot in all of his unassimilable heterogeneity, but which failed to mention the truncated portion of his bibliography—the 1930s right-wing journalism—that had only recently so shocked us both. (I have just returned from a memorial session for Derrida at Harvard in which his specific genius was nicely eulogized as an ability to confront thinking with what it seemed—constitutively— to exclude. Such was the tenor of my work on Blanchot, but such too the nub of my criticism of *Parages*.) In addition, I essayed a speculative genealogy. I proposed that Derrida be seen as the true heir of Jean Paulhan, whose death occurred more or less at the time of the publication of *De la grammatologie*. Paulhan, in his later years, had developed a linguistic principle of what he called "counter-identity," an interesting sequel to Freud's "Antithetical Sense of Primal Words," and something of an anticipation of

Derrida's *différance*. More interestingly still, Paulhan's principle came with a political coefficient. It will be recalled that Paulhan was a man of impeccable credentials in the Resistance, who, in the view of many, had somewhat muddied the ethical waters in the immediate postwar period. He did so by proposing that, since the core of the Resistance had spent the entire prewar period trampling on the French flag and preparing for its own *collaboration* with Moscow and the core of the Collaboration had spent the same years preparing for its own *resistance* against just such a collaboration, there was no basis for the Resistance to assume the moral high ground once the war was over. Such would be the principle of counter-identity in its political instantiation: as nice a chiasmus as any in deconstruction.

I shall skip over the extent of Derrida's anger over this piece (the canceled lecture at Berkeley, the hit list of "enemies of literary theory" in the form of a presidential address to the MLA by Hillis Miller). I have recounted the argument of "Writing and Deference" because of the role it played in my *Newsweek* interview. For I had assumed that the magazine would react to the de Man revelations with a wistful sense of the strangeness of it all: a great man with an unsavory past; how people do change . . . So conventional a perspective—which, in my naiveté I attributed to the weekly— seemed to me unworthy of deconstruction, obsessed as it productively was with the potential centrality of what all were prepared to consign to the margins. It seemed to me that the best way to press that case was to review the argument I had just made (and have here just encapsulated) in "Writing and Deference." There were speculative grounds, I claimed, for regarding the whole of deconstruction as a vast amnesty project for the politics of resistance and collaboration during World War II. The point, it will be seen, was to keep the chiastic crux at the heart of the historical tragedy. *Newsweek* cut out the word "speculative," and was perhaps right to do so: the editors recognized a rhetorical escape hatch when they saw one. But then a second excision was made. I was quoted as saying there were "grounds for viewing the whole of deconstruction as a vast amnesty project for the politics of collaboration during World War II."[4] In striking out "resistance," David Lehman, the journalist who would subsequently expand his article into a vengeful book, had removed the chiasmus, and turned my statement into a denunciation of deconstruction as so much political whitewash.

Once again, as with the earlier encounter with Searle, as with the *Times* obituary that left a number of people reeling, what was at stake was an inability to recognize the degree of hostility that Derrida's work, for all the currency given to the word "deconstruction," has tended to evoke. I suddenly perceived the folly of trying to summarize "Writing and Deference" to *Newsweek* and concluded that trying to right matters in a letter to the editor would only compound the morass. I assume that the magazine article sealed the disaffection felt by Derrida ever since "Writing and Deference." I was definitively out of the loop.

Some years later we met up at a Columbia celebration of the bicentenary of the Ecole normale supérieure (which happened to be the place, in 1968, at a reception in the anomalously posh director's residence, where we first met). We exchanged letters, mine going over some of the matters mentioned in these pages, his laced with references to a friendship that might have continued ("Si j'avais encore un conseil amical à donner"), which may have been an opening, or a reopening, but which was never pursued. Some years later, I came across his text on forgiveness: it argues the only thing worth pardoning is the unpardonable. I have occasionally wondered how my own story with him fit into that paradox. I will miss him, not least for the aporia that was our friendship.

Bellow in Boston

For the world he was Chicago incarnate, an idea-prone sensibility whose preferred idiom was a kind of street-wise downtown brashness. His friend Allan Bloom claimed that he was to Chicago what Balzac was to Paris. And Chicago was, in a way, the opposite of Paris for him. He had gone to the French capital in 1948 with the hope of writing what, in his milieu, was known by the acronym "G.A.N.": the "great American novel." And he more or less did it in the *Adventures of Augie March*. But the inspiration came to him as a visitation, on the banks of the Seine, from the American Midwest. There was a sudden realization that the voice of his forgotten Chicago friend Chucky, a "wild talker always announcing that he had a super scheme," would be the voice of his novel. And the voice wouldn't stop. "All I had to do was be there with buckets to catch it."[1]

As indigenous as he seemed to be to Chicago, he was not born there but in a suburb of Montreal, from which he could still remember the anti-Semitic taunts of his earliest childhood: "*maudit juif*," as he took pleasure in intoning in a marked Québecois accent. Nor did he die in Chicago. His last twelve years, during which I came to know him, were spent in Boston, where he taught, for as long as he could, at Boston University, where we were colleagues. I remember asking him, at our first dinner, why he stayed in Chicago all those years. His answer was pure Bellow: "I figured that by the time an idea made its way to Chicago, it would be so worn out that you could see straight through it." The wise-guy wit was irresistible. His was a world of conmen, and he had the spirit of a man intent on not being conned. Where others saw virtue, he could sense a "racket," and it made for some of his more unforgettable lines: "Her figleaf," as one of his characters sums up the charms of a mistress, "turned out to be a price tag."[2]

As for why he left Chicago, the answer was more brooding: he had become sick of passing by the houses of old friends who had died. And so, late in his seventies, he had picked up and brought his young wife (his fifth), the soon-to-be heroine of his final novel, *Ravelstein*, to New England. And perhaps because it was Boston and not Chicago, we came to talk mostly about matters French, as though Boston provided a measure of extraterritoriality in relation to Chicago, the city whose specificity, since the time of his epiphany on the Seine, was to be a kind of anti-Paris.

There was an irony in his coming to Boston University, since that institution had only recently become the home of *Partisan Review*, the initially left-wing journal of high literary modernism that had first welcomed him, but from which, following a negative review of *Herzog*, he was now estranged. His verdict on the opportunism of the journal, whose decease in Boston preceded Bellow's own by no more than a year, is worth recalling: "They want to cook their meals over Pater's 'hard gemlike flame' and light their cigarettes at it."[3]

He had his reservations, as his biographer reminds us, about university life. As a teacher, we are told, he was something of a "clock-watcher." Or as he put it to one of his charges at another university: "Just look at me as your friendly barber. I'll lather you, but you have to shave yourself." No doubt he sensed that, at bottom, the "professorial bit," as he put it, was "a marvelous racket."[4] Still, the passion of this "Chicago Dostoyevskian," as he called himself, for genuine achievements of the imagination was palpable.

His age, of course, fueled his skepticism. Philip Roth has described memorably the Chekhovian quality of his seventy-fifth birthday party in Vermont, where he kept a country home. "People got up and burst into tears and sat down."[5] It was years after that extraordinary event that the novelist arrived in Boston, and it is hard to imagine what enthusiasms might have survived it. I had a taste of his own bitter wisdom after giving him a recent book of mine, published in Chicago, as it happens, on the radio scripts for children written by Walter Benjamin. He wrote me back a generous letter, but whose memorable observations included: "I may as well admit that my patience with Benjamin's sort of Weimar culture has always been limited.

For this I blame myself. Not being a scholar I haven't the inclination to follow the esoteric intricacies of the notions he develops. And as the years go on I also think less and less kindly of Freud's analytical subtleties. My attitude seems to be, as I now consider it, that while we have to accommodate certain ideas or notions, we don't actually have to live by them. Influential as they may be, I let them sail by." The wisdom at which he had arrived perhaps found its most succinct formulation in a line from *Jerusalem and Back*: "A great deal of intelligence can be invested in ignorance when the need for illusion is deep."[6] There are lesser insights to live by.

He was more viscerally interested in a piece I wrote on the anti-Semitism of French intellectual life during the interwar years. A second letter informed me: "The one case that caused me the most pain was that of Paul Morand whose book on nightlife charmed me out of my shoes 40 years ago." Yes, one senses the affinities of Morand's jazzified prose with Bellow's, and senses the American's anguish at the particularly cruel anti-Jewish satire of *France-la-doulce*, which ends with an unprincipled Jewish film magnate, shortly before World War II, raising his glass in a toast to France, "God's own concentration camp."

Now that he is gone, though, let me not forget his wit—and its contagiousness. During his Boston years, the Sorbonne had elected to give him an honorary doctorate. Arrangements were made, and then Bellow went *incommunicado*. Since one of the arrangers of the honor was a friend of mine, I received an anguished phone call beseeching me to find out what was going on. I remember the difficulty of securing the phone number of his country getaway in Vermont, and then the wit of that voice on the answering machine: "How the hell did you find me? To tell you the truth, I'm surprised you did." The effect of that message was to open up an unknown Bellovian strain in my own voice. When I finally got him on the line, it was to say: "Saul, what's going on? The boys at the Sorbonne are getting antsy. They've already ordered the ermine and *you don't even answer?*" He must have enjoyed the shtick, because his comeback was perfection itself: "Will they pay for the ticket?" Then, of course: "Let me ask the Mrs." . . .

It was not the first occasion on which his doctors forbade travel. A year or so earlier I received a phone call, in which he told me that his doctors had discouraged him from traveling to Oxford to give a lecture And since I had always struck him as "an adventurous soul," he wanted to know whether I would be interested in going in his stead. Well, I may not have been the first to receive such a call from the master, but I was apparently the first to say yes to the request. And thus it was that I took off to Oxford, where I discovered to my mild horror that my audience had already paid a considerable sum for the pleasure of hearing the Nobel Prize winner. As I was heading toward the lecture hall, it occurred to me that Bellow's most recent novel, *The Actual*, dealt with a wily ninety-year-old Chicago Jew who maneuvers to send a younger man off on a mission as his surrogate—with all sorts of unexpected consequences. Might I and my audience not be characters in a Bellow fiction? I shared my thought with one of my hosts, the distinguished Oxford historian Keith Thomas, who chuckled and commented that I now had an ideal opening for my talk. I begged off, but in view of the audience's obvious torpor following a particularly tedious performance by P. D. James, my predecessor on the podium, I opted to begin my talk as suggested. The reaction was total silence. Thereafter I decided to ask Keith Thomas over dinner whether the silence signified that it was enough to mention the word "Jew" in the august precincts of Oxford for all possibility of laughter to be eliminated. The question was daring and I assumed that the historian would answer in the negative. In fact, he did not: "It may very well be the case."

*

When I first recounted the episode, for the Buenos Aires daily *La Nación*, shortly after Bellow's death, I was tempted to conclude with a provocative reference to Borges, the city's tutelary genius. It is a line that has always intrigued me but which I decided to cut from my text—a definition of the aesthetic per se as the imminence of a revelation that never comes. That thought resonates strangely with a proposition advanced by an author much admired by Borges, Léon Bloy, for whom the Jew and the Jew alone impedes the letter of the Old Testament in its transit toward fulfillment in the New. Combine the notions of Borges and Bloy, and it is almost as though anti-Semitism were the aesthetic sentiment par excellence. On that day in Oxford, I had a sense of a North American refutation of the Borges-Bloy proposition. For the most distinguished novelistic voice in the American twentieth century—that "mingling of high-flown intellectual bravado with racy-tough street Jewishness," as the critic Irving Howe put it—seemed on that occasion a triumphant reaction to no other sentiment than anti-Semitism itself.[7]

10

Antinomian Steiner

On a brilliant fall day in 1993, a year in which Newbury Street still managed to support a bookstore or two, I found myself strolling down that most urbane of Boston thoroughfares and stopping in at Waterstone's to browse. Once inside, I picked up the latest issue of the Times Literary Supplement and discovered to my surprise that it contained an article by George Steiner about Walter Benjamin, on whom I had published a slim volume a few months before. I opened the issue and, in my distraction, was suddenly brought up short at seeing that among the books the legendary critic was reviewing was my own "essay on his radio years," Walter Benjamin for Children. I quickly closed the paper. The day was too gorgeous, and Steiner too famously ornery, for me to want to have to deal with his misgivings amidst all that autumnal splendor. (Years earlier, as a visitor at Yale, he had been quick to dismiss an interpretation of Proust I had proposed to him as a graduate student.) I nonetheless bought the issue, stuffed it in my pocket, and later in the day had the pleasure of discovering that, although the article was characteristically hostile to the books it discussed, the one exception was my own, on which considerable praise was lavished.

I was able to meet and thank Steiner a few years later when he came as a guest speaker to the translation seminar I was conducting at Boston University. The fact that he was prepared to come—and mesmerize his audience—for a relatively modest sum marks a second subject of gratitude. (I suspect that a happy turn in my career at Boston University may have been a result of the administration's observation that the great man was coming at my invitation and

on my watch.) Finally, a third debt deserves mention: the remarkable transla-
tor, Pierre-Emmanuel Dauzat, whom Steiner and I share in France.

This "analysis in the form of a memoir," which deals with what I find
most troubling in the critic's work, is haunted by the intrusions of my own
identification with that very (antinomian) dimension. This chapter could,
that is, very easily have been shifted to the section "Semblables et frères." A
French version appeared in the issue of Cahiers de l'Herne *devoted to Steiner.*

*

A quintessential Steiner moment. The occasion was a lecture at MIT
during one of his almost annual visits to Boston that had quickened the
life of the city a few years back. The theme this time was "music-the-
language-that-cannot-lie." The audience, as usual, listened with rapt attention, but the felicitous moment I refer to came not during the lecture, but
the question period. A woman respectfully raised the subject of Wagner
as a counterexample. The implication was clear: the anti-Semitism of *Das*
Judentum in der Musik, the cult of the composer entertained by the Nazis,
must surely mark Wagner's accomplishment as fundamentally tainted by
one of the more malignant varieties of mendacity to have blemished European modernity. Whereupon the lecturer, in perfect tripartite cadence,
delivered himself of the introduction to the answer that interests me: "The
Lord has sent you" (and the questioner smiled as if receiving the benedic-
tion of her distinguished interlocutor) "into my hands" (and the audience
experienced a momentary squirm at the unexpected evocation of physical contact, still presumably beneficent, between lecturer and questioner)
"like the Amalekites." Whereupon this listener's jaw dropped, less at the
realization that a trap had been sprung than out of shock that in a context of genocide as cliché the speaker had, of a sudden and in the form of
a quip, affirmed his identity as a Jew, but less as the victim than as the perpetrator of a storied genocide.

That pleasure in a specifically Hebraic mode of cruelty was a touch
not totally unfamiliar to the reader of Steiner. A memorable "preface" to the
Hebrew Bible describes Joshua as "the least attractive text in the canon. It records tribal arrogance and cruelty with undoubted relish."[2] And in "Totem
or Taboo": "The Book of Joshua is one of the cruelest books ever written; it
is a book of savagery."[3] When penned by the abbé Pierre, just such thoughts,
be they true or false, would issue, in France, in a wholesale accusation of

anti-Semitism, the last sputterings of the Vichy syndrome.[4] But here they were expressed by one of the principal memorialists of the Nazi genocide, a development as unexpected as the Amalekite quip with which we began.

And to which we return. For that introduction to a response turned out to resonate with the answer it introduced. The lecturer proceeded to evoke a memorable turn-of-the-century performance of Wagner in Vienna. In the orchestra sat Theodor Herzl; in one of the higher balconies sat—or stood—Adolf Hitler. The two were said to have been equally inspired by the performance but no doubt to have dreamt very different dreams. Chronology may pose a bit of a problem here. Hitler's assiduous attendance at Wagner performances at the Vienna Court Opera, as reported by his friend Kubizek, lasted from February to July 1908; he was nineteen at the time.[5] Herzl, however, had died in 1906. We are, in sum, dealing with a Steinerian myth of music, a genre that has long interested him. There is something of "elemental inhumanity," he suggests in *Errata*, in the condition of a language bereft of reference.[6] Whence the "inhuman" violence of the myths— Marsyas flayed, Orpheus dismembered, the murderous Sirens—that he associates with the origins of music. But "beyond true and false," the burden of the nonreferential, brings him to "beyond good and evil," and it is there that his Wagner myth is grounded: Hitler and Herzl, Nazi and Jew, perpetrator and victim, communing, unthinkably, in the fathomless music of the future.

Like the Amalekites . . .

*

One reason the Amalekite quip, which might well have been dismissed as a throwaway line, has stayed with me is that it resonated so surprisingly with a chapter on Steiner that I had just completed for a volume on French émigrés in New York City during World War II.[7] Indeed, since much of what I shall present in these pages is on the order of an expansion of that chapter, it may be well to elucidate that resonance as I then perceived it.

The connection is most explicit in relation to Steiner's principal work of fiction, the novella *The Portage to San Cristobal of A.H.* The subject, it will be recalled, is the panic unleashed in a series of Western capitals at the thought of a war crimes trial for a quaking ninety-year-old Adolf Hitler, captured by the Israeli secret service in the Amazon jungle. For the varieties of compromise with the incarnation of evil of which each of the putative enemies of Nazism had been guilty can only issue in some particularly embarrassing moments for them all. What is of particular interest in the present context, however, is the end of the novella, which consists of a speech delivered by Hitler, his first words in the book, to his Israeli captors. Its theme is that he learned his every trick from the Jews: "From you. Everything. To set a race apart. To keep it from defilement. To hold before it a promised land. To scour that land of its inhabitants or place them in servitude. Your beliefs. Your arrogance. . . . My racism was a parody of yours, a hungry imitation."[8] Now, what is most striking is that Hitler's concluding speech receives no rebuttal. The novella concludes, that is, much as the Amalekite quip did: the putative victims of genocide, the Jews, are assigned responsibility at some level for inventing the genre. Wagner, culture at its most exalted, is the medium in which Herzl and Hitler can commune. It is a proposition, I have argued, right out of Simone Weil: Hitler, the apotheosis of Rome (Weil's "great atheistic beast"), and Israel (her "great religious beast") were twin cultural formations.[9]

Now, the extent of the compatibility or incompatibility of Rome and Jerusalem, it turns out, is the theme of the single literary work to which Steiner, in *Errata*, attributes his literary vocation: Racine's *Bérénice*. For it was the "immense minimalism" of the Racine play, studied at the Lycée français of wartime New York, that initiated the young reader into the "long noon of French literature" and kindled his will to serve as a comparatist—that is, a virtuoso of "double or triple agency," the noble or "honest treason" of espousing and elucidating cultural values deemed to be other than one's own.[10] *Bérénice*, of course, is a drama about the consequences of a war against the Jews. At the time of the destruction of the Second Temple, Titus takes on a Jewish concubine, Bérénice, but is obliged to dismiss her—*invitus invitam*, against his will and hers, in Suetonius's phrase—once he ascends to the august rank of emperor. To the extent that the departure of Bérénice, the dismissal of the Jew, has been read as more *invitam* than *invitus*, one is tempted to read the play itself—or to allegorize the experience of reading it during World War II—in terms of the Jewish policies of the Vichy regime as analyzed by the historians Robert Paxton and Michael Marrus: an allegedly involuntary (*invitus*) deportation and/or persecution of France's Jews that was on occasion pursued with a zeal that seems anything but involuntary.[11]

More striking still is the extent to which the very subject of Bérénice seems awash in "double agency." Bérénice herself, concubine of her people's conqueror, was vulnerable to imputations of betrayal. And our principal historical source for the myth is Josephus, the Jewish historian whose opposition to the zealotry of those resisting Rome had sent him into the camp of the Romans. So that Steiner's path into the "honest treason" of comparative literature seems haunted by an "honest treason" bent on the phantasm of a union binding Jew and anti-Jew: Bérénice and Titus, Jerusalem and Rome, Moses and A.H., Herzl and Hitler, Hebrew and Amalekite.

*

Wagner, the "Alpine chain" constituted by his *oeuvre*, we have seen, would appear to be the talismanic composer for Steiner.[12] And yet the opera he chose to comment on at intriguing length in his first volume of essays, *Language and Silence*, was not Wagnerian but Schönberg's unfinished masterpiece *Moses und Aron*. Not that Wagner is absent from the piece. Steiner is careful to state that it is inexact to say that the opera is "without precedent," since it is "related to Wagner's *Parsifal*."[13] Thus we are again confronted, however peripherally, with the relation between Wagner—or opera per se—and Judaism. The composer wrote in a letter to Alban Berg that the work was a crucial part of his "return to Judaism."[14]

Schönberg's conceit pits Aaron, whose propensity to idolatry is figured in part by his glorious voice, against Moses, whose role is spoken rather than sung. The askesis demanded by a God said to be *unvorstellbar*, unrepresentable, thus dictates a sacrifice of song, the quintessential property of opera, itself. Steiner relates this Mosaic sacrifice to the circumstance that ultimately led to Schönberg's failure to complete the opera. He agrees with Adorno that the work was conceived in part as a "preventive action against the looming of Nazism."[15] And yet history was conspiring to arrange a strange contamination of the libretto by that which it was nominally predicated against: "The words *Volk* and *Führer* figure prominently in the opera; they designate its supreme historical values, Israel and Moses. Now they were wrested out of Schoenberg's grasp by the millions bawling them at Nuremberg. How could he continue to set them to music?"[16] But the conflation of Moses and Hitler, *Führer* and *Führer*, which is presented as an unfortunate contingency in the essay, corresponds precisely to the phantasm, a virtual wish-fulfillment, that concludes *The Portage to San*

Cristobal: "Your invention. One Israel, one *Volk*, one leader," as A.H. puts it. It is as though what was *unvorstellbar*, unrepresentable, was, for Steiner, less the abstract God of the Jews than a certain undecidability between the Hebrews and their fiercest adversaries.

*

(And I am reminded of the most eloquent put-down I have ever received. Steiner had read an essay of mine no doubt inspired in part by what I had subliminally perceived in his work and have been attempting to give voice to in these pages.[17] At issue was the sinister subtext supplied by history for Exodus: the emergency gathering of the Hebrews amidst the midnight howls occasioned by the Tenth Plague; the announcement, by a leader plainly raised among their enemies, that they would in short order be resettled in the distant East; the "murmurings" of the resentful Hebrews; the extravaganza of the Golden Calf, whose astonishing intricacy in the Schönberg setting Steiner commented on; and then the massacre ordered up by Moses, right there in the "camp," amidst the mysterious smoke billowing up from Sinai. Might the dream of Sinai, I found myself wondering, not at some level be pregnant with the principal nightmare of recent Jewish history? It is, I hope to have demonstrated, the Steinerian question par excellence. Whence the interest of the brio with which he deflected it—with what was said to be François Mauriac's memorable reaction to a reading of a novel by Graham Greene: "Catholicism, you should be aware, is something extremely complicated; but it is not as complicated as that . . .").

*

The piece on the Moses opera has the value of a signature. For the Biblical patriarch, as conceived by the composer, is said to be less a reminder (or heir) of Michelangelo than of Alban Berg's *Wozzeck*: "Moses and Wozzeck are both brilliant studies in dramatic contradiction, operatic figures unable to articulate with the fullness of their own voices the fullness of their needs and perceptions."[18] But for the Steiners *Woyzeck* was a heraldic text: "My great-grandfather made the chance discovery, in a drugstore in the Galician town of Landberg, of Büchner's play, *Woyzeck*. Although no one knew the text's value, with full confidence in his writerly judgment, he published it, realizing that he was dealing with a masterpiece. Even today, I consider that saving that text from oblivion is a title of nobility for our family."[19]

Our interpretation of Steiner's reading of *Moses und Aron*—the "unrepresentable," which is to say the musical per se, linked less to one of the two terms in a conflict than to the inability to establish a separation between them—receives odd confirmation in the essay that follows the Schönberg development in *Language and Silence*. It is entitled "A Kind of Survivor" and is dedicated to Elie Wiesel. It is, that is, a key text on the Nazi genocide of the Jews and an early statement on just how relentlessly it weighed on a Jewish intellectual's sense of self: "The black mystery of what happened in Europe is to me indivisible from my own identity. Precisely because I was not there."[20] Now, at its most specific, Steiner's sense of the post-Hitlerian Judaic relates to a particular form of helplessness in the face of a threat lodged against one's child: "The sense I have of the Jew as a man who looks on his children with a dread remembrance of helplessness and an intimation of future murderous possibility, is a very personal, isolated one."[21] Infanticide would appear to mark the unspeakable core of genocide.

That observation takes on particular saliency when one turns to a short story by Steiner entitled "A Conversation Piece" and dedicated to an almost Kabbalistic discussion of the binding of Isaac, conducted by Jews in a gas chamber just prior to the releasing of "the slurred slow song of gas."[22] Might Abraham, it is asked, not have mistaken the voice of Satan, commanding him to the unthinkable, for the voice of God? But the debate reaches its most searing point in conclusion: "No Jewish son looks on his father without remembering that he may be sacrificed by his father's hand."[23] For it is as though the fiction had culminated by turning the helpless victim—or witness—of an unimaginable crime in "A Kind of Survivor" into its potential perpetrator. Precisely as the doomed Mosaic affirmation against the Nazis in the essay on Schönberg modulated, by way of fiction, into A.H.'s concluding affirmation of the ultimate indistinguishability between the two.

And once again the entire process is accompanied by chords out of Wagner. From "A Kind of Survivor": Jewish consciousness "recognized in Wagner the radicalism and histrionic tactics of a great outsider. It caught in Wagner's anti-Semitism a queer, intimate note, and gave occasional heed to the stubborn myth that Wagner was himself of Jewish descent."[24] Is not the myth of Herzl and Hitler dreaming to Wagner at the same Viennese performance already here in the evocation of a fantasy of Wagner as Jewish in his very anti-Semitism?

*

The binding of Isaac is a focus of what is perhaps the climactic—and strangest—of encounters between anti-Semite and Jew in Steiner's *oeuvre*, the volume titled *Dialogues* which he published in 1994 with the philosopher Pierre Boutang. Boutang was the sometime secretary of Charles Maurras, sometime pamphleteer against the Jews, the fair-haired boy of French fascism who never recovered from the encomium he received from Lucien Rebatet in his arch-collaborationist *Les Décombres*, and the author, according to Steiner, of one of the major philosophical texts of the twentieth century, *L'Ontologie du secret*.[25] Perhaps the oddity of their dialogue— or friendship—is best captured in the two subtexts evoked by Steiner as the informing conceits of their conversation. On the one hand, the absolute of friendship: the *parce-que-c'était-lui-parce-que-c'était-moi* that was Montaigne's sole explanation of his affection for La Boétie.[26] On the other: "C'est à l'image des deux statues au portail de la cathédrale de Strasbourg, l'une de l'Eglise triomphante mais étrangement floue, l'autre d'une Synagogue brisée, les yeux bandés mais, elle, étrangement tenace, que je vis nos rencontres."[27] Rome—the Rome of Boutang's militant Catholicism—and Jerusalem (of Steiner the Jew) enter into a relation of passionate commitment that is also one of painful subjugation. (Just how painful may be intuited from the fact that in the presumably more controlled English of the memoir *Errata*, an effort has been made to mask the extent of the subjugation: "At one of the portals of the Cathedral of Strasburg, Synagogue, blindfolded, and Church, compassionate yet regal, confront each other across an abyss of unhoused hope."[28] Both *brisée* and *triomphante* have been excised from the text.) It is the simultaneity of the impassioned mutuality and the devastating defeat (of Jerusalem by Rome, Synagogue by Church), the stuff of the tutelary myth of Bérénice and Titus, that is, I believe, at the vexed core of the dialogue.

But the exchange began not with Bérénice but with Antigone. Steiner, in admiration of *L'Ontologie du secret*, had dedicated a copy of his *Antigones* to the Frenchman as follows: "Pour Pierre Boutang, allié, mais infidèle de Créon."[29] The implication was that Boutang, a man of order like Creon, was plainly slated to be on the side of collaboration, but that his inherent superiority would have made him incapable of fulfilling that catastrophic role.[30] Boutang's incensed reply was not long in coming. Not only was his master Maurras a lifelong devotee of Antigone herself (Creon being at best a Bonapartist, not a Bourbon), but to the extent that he, Boutang, himself had sacrificed an academic career in order to fight the good fight for an honorable burial for Pétain, he was far more an avatar of Antigone than of her lamentable uncle. Thus it was over a crisscrossed interpretation of the modern valences of the myth of Antigone that the Steiner-Boutang dialogue was launched.

But it was over the binding of Isaac that things came to a head. For the subject—of sacrifice and survival—is in perpetual contact, for Steiner, with the Shoah. Toward the close of the discussion, we read:

G.S.: At the beginning of our dialogue, our discussion, and it has not been easy, Boutang—
P.B.: It's not over yet!
G.S.: —I paid tribute, and with all my heart and soul, to what it is that I so deeply love in you, which is your courage. But have the courage, good God, to admit that for you the disappearance of the Jew would finally be—
P.B.: The opposite of what I think
G.S.: —the validation of what is both in the Epistle to the Romans—

Boutang reacts with horror, as though he had been lured into a trap: "Your question is disobliging. . . . It requires me to tell you that it is false! That on my word and on my honor, it is false. That at no time, moreover, could I have wished, or could anyone have wished for the destruction of anything participating in the realm of spirit."[31] Steiner, having all but confessed earlier in the dialogue that a feeling of physical subjugation was inseparable from whatever bound him to Boutang, asks the Frenchman to have the decency to admit wherein the theological dimension of his will to domination—"la Synagogue brisée"—might lie. Boutang demurs and the dialogue comes to a close amidst evasive pieties about shared investments in theology.

*

But Steiner's question was on the mark. Moreover, Boutang had offered an answer chilling in its pertinence years earlier in a commentary on Gabriel Marcel's play *Le Signe de la croix.* He called it "Une tragédie du judaïsme." What renders the Marcel play chilling in this context is that it offers a view of the fate of a Jewish family of Viennese origin, residing in

Paris at the outbreak of World War II and forced to decide whether to seek refuge, in the face of persecution, in the United States. Its situation, that is, was almost precisely that of the Steiner family as evoked in various interviews and the memoir *Errata*.

Boutang evokes Marcel's play as the drama of a Jew who has come to see the wisdom of the "state anti-Semitism" of Maurras. Simon Bernauer, the protagonist, is a Jew, a music lover and record producer, a reader of (if not a subscriber to) *Action française*, and the uneasy husband of Pauline, whom Boutang describes as a "ridiculous" and "odious" *Juive de choc*.[32] Specifically, what is taken by Boutang to be "ridiculous" is Pauline's indignation upon learning that her talented brother Léon has been denied entry—in 1938—to medical school, despite his obvious excellence, because he is a Jew. What is regarded as "odious" is the "precipitation with which she advises him to leave for America."[33] For surely, Boutang suggests, it is odious to love France only for what she can bring to one in the way of a career.

With the arrival of the war, Simon grows increasingly attached to a self-effacing aunt (Lena) from Vienna. Meanwhile, his son David—whom Boutang dismisses as "scholastically, unbearably Jewish (close to Proust's character Bloch)"—is taken to Drancy and presumably killed after he refuses to be intimidated by the Germans and sports his yellow star at a performance of Bach he insists on attending in occupied Paris.[34] Transformed by the suffering he sees around him, Simon dispatches his wife and other son to America and chooses to die with the Jews around him, having learned the meaning of Christian sacrifice, rather than choose a "vain exile" in America. His final words, we eventually learn, are a pardon for a notorious collaborator who had chosen to facilitate Pauline's departure for America.

The play, in sum, as read by Boutang, is an emphatic confirmation of what was implied by Steiner's plea to Boutang in the *Dialogues*: "But have the courage, good God, to admit that for you the disappearance of the Jew would finally be . . ." For Boutang, like Maurras, indeed like the sometime sympathizer of Action Française Gabriel Marcel, would consign the Jew—in search, like Léon, of an exemplary life—to an exemplary death. It is Simon's choice to eschew vulgar exile in America and to renew the mystery of Christian sacrifice by dying in solidarity with the persecuted he had until then scorned. Everything else is either "ridiculous and odious" (in the case of Pauline) or "scholastically, unbearably Jewish" (in that of David, who refuses to let the Nazi "brutes" deprive him of attendance at the Concerts Colonne).

It is the points of contact with the saga of the family Steiner that are perhaps most gripping. Vienna-Paris-America: the prospect or reality of a double exile within which both dramas are played out. On the one hand, Léon, unable to carry all the prizes garnered at the *distribution des prix* of Janson-de-Sailly.[35] On the other, Steiner, referring to the same lycée as "the hub of our intellectual radiance."[36] Finally, the bizarre circumstance that led Steiner père to do precisely what Boutang and Marcel praised Simon Bernauer for *not* doing: in Manhattan, negotiating the purchase of Grumman aircraft for the French Foreign Ministry during the *drôle de guerre*, Steiner père is accosted by an old German business acquaintance on a similar mission on behalf of the Germans; he tells Steiner that the killing has already begun in the East and persuades him to get his family out of France as soon as possible.[37] Without which initiative, among other things, the inconceivability of these words of tribute.

Primary masochism, the later Freud would have it, takes matters as far as they can go. The Steiner friendship—"might it finally be more than friendship?"[38]—for Boutang, Steiner has said, partakes of a kind of "self-disdaining fascination."[39] Is it not as though Steiner, in his relation with Boutang, had touched on that Freudian ultimate? In an important text titled "Logocrats," Steiner offers a rare intellectual lineage: Joseph de Maistre, Martin Heidegger, Pierre Boutang. What is striking in the essay is that, whereas the author is at his most characteristically eloquent and insightful on Heidegger and Maistre, when it comes to the final member of his trio, discussing Boutang's masterwork, *L'Ontologie du secret*, he seems oddly at a loss: "I am by no means confident that I have rightly grasped or that I can adequately paraphrase cardinal points in Boutang's study of the active presence of 'what is secret,' of 'what is phenomenally absent from' human utterance."[40] This sense of felicitous defeat by the text, of "privileged servitude" in relation to language, is oddly apposite since such is the specific domain—or theme—of "logocracy" itself: man the uneasy intruder in the "house of language."[41] That this passion for the dimension of "uneasy intrusion" should mesh so precisely with the motif of the Jew's uneasy intrusion in the house of France, as discussed by its exemplary thinker, is a circumstance that may give us pause.

*

*And of a sudden I recall my own initiation into the world of French
letters. As a first-year undergraduate at Harvard in 1961, I recall peering out
of my dormitory room window in Matthews South. We were all freshmen
in Harvard Yard, yet I was greeted regularly by the spectacle of an aged and
portly gentleman preparing his nightly toilette in the freshman dormitory directly across the path from mine. I finally discovered that the aged gentleman
who unknowingly, anomalously, accompanied me in that first year of studying
French letters was Gabriel Marcel, then a visiting professor, whose attitude toward the path a Jew such as myself had taken I have had to wait until now,
writing about George Steiner, to discover.*

*It was a memorable first year at Harvard, a first plunge into the world
of French letters—pursued so far from that secret center of French thought, as
Boutang would have it, Gabriel Marcel's apartment on the rue de Tournon—
a year perched high over Harvard Yard, though not many yards from my secret
sharer in Grays Hall, Gabriel Marcel himself. Inspired—or intimidated—
into excellence by the eminence of the institution, as "scolairement, insupport-
ablement juif," no doubt, as Boutang's version of Marcel's David, I was among
those given a prize at year's end, a book of my choice to be bound and inscribed.
Detur, "that it be given," was the name of the prize, and I have occasionally
thought of it in Germanic, indeed Heideggerian, terms: Sei es gegeben, that
something be given, ait lieu. The gift of a sign under which a life of thought
would be pursued. Denken, danken, thinking as thanking, in Heidegger's
pun. And Steiner, at the end of his memorable monograph on the philosopher:
"There are meaner metaphors to live by."[42]*

*The problem, of course, was to choose a book. With time running out,
I opted for Santayana's "memoir in the form of a novel,"* The Last Puritan.
*It was an influential high school teacher who had promoted Santayana, that
"Español emersonizado," as Borges called him, as the gold standard. And the
quality of the prose convinced me the choice was right.*

*Or was it the prospect of the tragedy of "last (or ultimate) Puritanism"—
the American version of Vienna's "primary masochism"?—that attracted me
to the volume? Santayana, a name I have never seen discussed in French . . .
until I happened on the essay in* Les Abeilles de Delphes, *the volume by Boutang containing the scary reading of the Marcel play on the fate of the Jews.
And, to be sure, Boutang went right for what to me loomed as the essence:*

"the Jews, concerning whom he gives us a profound and terrifying analysis, not lacking in sympathy."[43] *The tone was unmistakable. As in the piece on Marcel, the essay that answers,* avant la lettre, *Steiner's plea in* Dialogues *to such devastating effect, the message is: Would that the Jews, through their actions, allowed me to think less harshly of them. And immediately, the anti-Jewish eloquence out of Santayana came streaming back to me. From* Reason in Religion: *The "crime" of the Jews is "to have denied the equal prerogative of other nations' laws and deities, for this they did, not from critical insight or intellectual scruples, but out of pure bigotry, conceit, and stupidity."*[44] *And the reference, in* Persons and Places, *to "all the Jews I have known, . . . inconsolably envious in their prosperity and profoundly vindictive in their humanitarianism."*[45] *Boutang on Santayana, in sum, through whom "it (will) be given" (*detur*), opening floodgates every bit as devastating for me as Boutang on Marcel deserved to be for George Steiner.*

*

Where Boutang, to whom Steiner led me, affected most directly the Bessarabian Jew at two generations' remove that I am, however, was in his postwar polemical pamphlet *La République de Joinovici.* "Un Juif de Bessarabie vient en France . . ."[46] Boutang would forge a myth of the degeneration of France under the Fourth Republic in terms of the arrival on French soil of Joinovici, a Bessarabian (and thus "stateless") Jew in 1925. Before long we find him playing both ends against the middle, selling trucks to the Gestapo but also militating (without risk) on behalf of the Resistance. That lack of principle—collaborator and *résistant,* the very emblematization of the civil war France had just undergone during the war—will earn him his credentials as the exemplary figure of the Fourth Republic, the 1940s' counterpart to Stavisky in the previous decade. But if Stavisky and Joinovici offer "parallel lives" in Boutang's burlesque *Impromptu de Bessarabie* (as he calls it), it is because his very text prides itself on its own parallelism with a sequence of prior texts, specifically as the culmination (or continuation) of a tradition that takes us from Edouard Drumont to Georges Bernanos to Boutang himself.

For *La République de Joinovici* is obsessed with its relation to *La Grande peur des bien-pensants,* Bernanos's celebrated biography in praise of the godfather of French anti-Semitism, Edouard Drumont. Specifically, it would rescue Bernanos from the antifascist (and in particular, anti-

Francoist) turn that he had taken with *Les Grands cimetières sous la lune.* The "drama" of Bernanos was to have been taken "hostage" by the philo-Semites, a circumstance now to be undone.[47] Joinovici was the reincarnation of Arthur Meyer, the "chand d'habits" become major newspaper publisher who is so heartlessly lampooned in *La Grande peur des bien-pensants.* Indeed, France itself, la *France juive*, had become "la Meyérie," a world that had effected the dreaded conflation of *l'Honneur* and *la Police* that Bernanos had warned about.[48]

*

And I recalled that the movement from the anti-Semitism of Drumont through the reversal—from fascist to antifascist—in Bernanos to the relentlessly philo-Semitic (but structurally congruent) problematic of Maurice Clavel and the "nouveaux philosophes" had furnished me with a kind of Möbius strip, a topological space within which to assess such enigmas as the evolution of the thought of, say, Maurice Blanchot (from the fascist-activist stance of the 1930s *Combat* to the "passivity beyond all passivity" of his postwar writings on "literary space").[49] It was the Möbian twist, I had concluded, that had authorized—for better or worse—the textual turns and hijinks of what had flourished as deconstruction. And here was Boutang stating that the Drumont-Bernanos-Clavel twist, far from furnishing the a priori space within which matters intellectual (and specifically textual) might alone be thought, was a perversion to be redressed and righted. If anti-Semitism had to all appearances become unspeakable, as Sartre suggested, in postwar France, if "Jewish fascism" had succeeded in turning the expression of anti-Semitic sentiments, the infraction of "lèse-juif," into the last taboo, then it was time for a genuine rollback or counterrevolution. For the Möbius strip conjoining the trio Drumont-Bernanos-Clavel, one must struggle to substitute the unyielding ramrod armature of Drumont-Bernanos-Boutang. The very same words of Maurras in defense of an "antisémitisme d'Etat" are cited in the essay on Marcel's play and in the pamphlet against "le Bessarabien lui-même."[50]

Whence the impatience with the "philosophical funambulism" under which term Boutang came to denounce deconstruction.[51] It is a phrase which resonates perfectly with the reference to "the circus-folk of deconstruction" in Steiner's *Errata.*[52] If deconstruction is one of the intellectual possibilities opened up by a discursive universe in which a fundamentally anti-Semitic configuration (Drumont-Bernanos I) comes to survive as a mode of philo-Semitism (Bernanos II-Clavel et al.), then there would be little room for it in the world of *La République de Joinovici,* one in which the anti-Semitic configuration (Drumont-Bernanos) is maintained in its sorry purity—be it against a Bernanos "embarrassed, constrained to bow and scrape before democracy and the Jews"—by the rhetoric of Boutang himself.[53] There was, it may be recalled, a violent debate between Boutang and Clavel on the future of France in the pages of *La Nation française* on October 10, 1956.[54]

Toward the end of *Dialogues,* just after the violent plea or challenge to Boutang that we have commented on, matters are defused by a reference to theology. In Steiner's words: "But there is something that binds us deeply. For two hours, we have been talking seriously about texts and the question: can one read without speaking about the existence or the role of God? We are in perfect agreement. And that isolates us, I think."[55] Before long the communion in a theology (or antitheology) of culture modulates to the supreme case, the thought of Walter Benjamin, become the very medium of their friendship.

Which leads me, with particular thought of the kind words George Steiner has written on my own short volume on Benjamin, to consider the metaphors selected by Boutang to discuss his arch villain, the Jew out of Bessarabia and bane of France, Joinovici.[56] He is, for Boutang, above all "le chiffonnier," the ragpicker, indeed "notre chiffonnier national."[57] At the same time, Boutang makes much of Joinovici's code name in the Resistance: Spaas, which is Russian for "savior."[58] The ragpicker, or *Lumpensammler,* as messiah: Boutang, in his screed, has alighted on precisely what Benjamin's most astute readers have identified as a commanding metaphor of the Arcades Project.[59] In order to pour his contempt on it.

For the *chiffonnier-sauveur* is part of a series of abject foreign Jews French literature at midcentury took pleasure in despising. Already in the Marcel play we have commented on, we are treated to an abject German Jew named Frosch, an obscene version of Kurt Weill, whom Simon delights in ejecting from his home. Simon's commentary (as quoted by Boutang): "You were speaking of France a moment ago, but you don't see that it has just been delivered over to this vermin."[60] To which one might link the bandit, a Galician Jew and last surviving virtuoso of "poetic" Yiddish, whom Zelten condemns to death in the first version of Giraudoux's play *Siegfried.*[61] Or the fraudulent moviemaker, Max Kron, in Paul Morand's

France-la doulce. Arriving in Paris from Berlin, drawn to the dream potential of the dying Paris arcades, then escaping from France by way of the
Pyrenees, with the unfinished draft of a "great" Germano-Jewish summa
on a certain essence of France—his film version of *La Chanson de Ro-
land*—under his arm, Kron, enacting a defeat of French probity at the
hands of Ashkenazi corruption, appears to be anticipating key elements of
Walter Benjamin's existence as they might have been dreamt by a French
anti-Semite.[62]

Which brings us back to Boutang and his exemplary Jew, Joinovici,
ragpicker and savior. Once again, the literary rhetoric of French Jew-hatred
at its most distinguished appears to parody the discourse (or situation) of
Benjamin. These remarks, then, part analysis, part memoir, in the hope
that George Steiner's retreat, toward the end of *Dialogues*, from his challenge to Boutang into what looms as a kind of *pax benjaminiana* will prove
in some measure more difficult.

11

A Professor Retires

*Derrida (from the time of our meeting in 1968 at the Ecole normale su-
périeure), Bellow (from the time that United Synagogue Youth, in the 1950s,
distributed a pamphlet by Leslie Fiedler to the effect that if you were a bright
Jewish kid, you'd better start reading literature, and there was no better place
to start than with Bellow's novels), and Steiner (from the time I first picked up
the New Yorker) each exercised an influence on me, but none was my teacher
per se. Such was not the case for Victor Brombert, with whom I had the privilege to study at Yale. What follows is a reminiscence of those Yale years as I wrote
them up in a letter to him on his retirement. It was incorporated in a collective volume of tribute and presented to him in 1999, in Princeton, at a party
in his honor.*

*

Dear Victor,

I am, as you may imagine, honored to have been called on for this
collective salute to you on your retirement.

My contribution to the festivities will be a few reminiscences that
have remained with me, lo these thirty years, of the Yale department you
chaired. It was, we were all convinced, *the* place to study French. The rub
was just how to do it. Yale, under your expert stewardship, was a high
temple of literary thematics. The visits of Georges Poulet and Jean-Pierre
Richard, among others, were particularly memorable, but somehow what I
remember above all of those visits was Richard's choice for lunch on the day

we dined—was it at Casey's?—on the New Haven Green. "*Poulet désossé*," said he, and it was surely as lapidarily precise an evocation of the work of the grand master of the Text Iridescent as any it has received. All this to say that the Signifier Serendipitous was already raising its Janus-head and that some of us, for all our admiration, were already, under the rubric "structuralism," looking for something (*soyons thématiciens!*) a bit *bonier*.

For my part, I recall, I was deeply convinced that structuralism would not have triumphed in New Haven (such was your centrality) until I (such was my naiveté) had converted you to it. Flaubert, thanks to your seminar, was very much in the air in those years, and I still remember the shock of a classmate, intrigued by the importance I attached to persuading you, when I cut him short with the words, "Mais Victor Brombert, c'est moi."

(In retrospect, I suppose, Madame Bovary did not descend on New Haven with a vengeance until years after both of us had left. The real danger, it has seemed to me, was that a generation of scholars and aspiring deconstructors, coming posthumously upon de Man's wartime journalism a bit as Charles Bovary did Emma's love letters, would soon subside into the same resigned indifference or spiritual lifelessness as the lamentable Charles.)

But there was also, of course, Stendhal. If there was a Brombert mystique, it was in part because we sensed that for all your passionate attachment to matters French, you had access to a transcendental realm beyond it. You called it Italy. Yours was no doubt an intuition somewhat on the order of Galbraith's in his suggestion that all his economic strictures did not hold for Italy, which managed to supersede them by dint of sheer style and inventiveness. It may indeed have been your access to that transcendental realm that led me to learn Italian, around a small table, reading Ariosto with Bart Giamatti (although I lost a good deal of it, around the same table, reading Tasso; for me, the charms of the Counter-Reformation did not come until later, with the seminars of Lacan). Or perhaps the "beyond French literature" some of us were searching for in structuralism was what we imagined you enjoying—blissfully—under the name of Italy.

All of which sounds a bit Oedipal and leads me to recall that these were the late sixties and revolt was in the air. Let me close, then, with a final reminiscence, which dates from 1969. I was at the Ecole normale. You were on leave in Paris, but agreed to meet with me for a drink at the Rhumerie martiniquaise. I remember the busload of armed police across the boulevard Saint-Germain, my sense that we were surely on the brink of something momentous. You deflected my every reference to the bus across the road with ever more insightful comments about *Le Nozze di Figaro* (or was it *Don Giovanni*?), insisting that that alone was what mattered.

Who, thirty years later, is to say you weren't right?

I wish you well, Victor.

Yours faithfully,

J. M.

STUDENTS

Genet in New Haven:
Repercussions and Resonances

At Yale, during the turbulent second half of the sixties, an almost hallu-cinatory intervention by an author I was teaching provides a perspective for a discussion of his oeuvre . . .

*

"And why not a book?" Arafat is quoted as asking Genet sometime during one of the writer's three stays with the Palestinians.[1] The answer was "Bien sûr," and the result the very remarkable volume called *Un captif amoureux*. Edmund White has compared that work, in its will to lyricize the aspirations of a dispossessed people, to nothing less than the Bible.[2] François Regnault calls it "a small epic," and then "the greatest novel to have been written in a long time."[3] The book, six hundred pages in length, which was preceded by a shorter text, "Quatre heures à Chatila," marked a return to literature for Genet, after thirty years of relative sterility, a re-discovery of his aesthetic vocation, and a last will and testament of sorts. He died while correcting proof.

But it is an odd personal resonance of the question posed by Arafat that I would like to comment on. In 1970, some years before Arafat popped his question, it was my curious fortune to be teaching Sartre's *Saint Genet* at Yale when Jean Genet showed up in New Haven, escorted by a phalanx of Black Panthers, and aggressively coaxed—or hustled—the Yale student body into not attending classes until Bobby Seale, then on trial for murder, received justice. Genet's Panther years were a kind of dress rehearsal for his Palestinian period, and the New Haven event is the subject of some rather striking pages in *Un captif amoureux*. (In order to set the stage for what will follow, I should say that years later I would again undergo the experience of having a lecture on a major French author interrupted or intercepted by the author in question, Maurice Blanchot, in ways that will have a bearing on what will follow.)[4] Let me return to the Genet episode, though. I remember showing up at the assembly called by Genet and the Panthers with my students and quite a few others, where we were roundly insulted by the Panthers. Here is Genet's version of the Panther discourse to the Yale community: "We don't begin by opposing your arguments with counter-arguments, but with sneers and insults. . . . We are out to outrage you and only later will we speak with you. When you are beaten down, broken, we will then calmly offer our arguments. Calmly and sovereignly" (359–360). My own recollection was embarrassment at the specific insult the Panthers reserved for the Yalies: "sissies," perhaps "faggots." All this as Jean Genet eyed them with a kind of erotic excitement that the pages of *Un captif amoureux* make no secret of. It was about then that I marshaled about as much truculence as a Yale graduate student in French could muster and shouted out a question to Genet (I blush to say it must have been in French): "All of us are, of course, convinced of the importance of what you're doing here. But when will you set it all down in writing?" Once a French professor, always a French professor. My question was, I suppose, the same as Arafat's, but it was plainly premature and coming from the wrong source. I still remember the look of fury with which Genet turned away from me. Years later I would recognize that contempt in the comments of another French author in an analogous circumstance. Here is Romain Gary's evocation of Marlon Brando voicing his own truculent solidarity with the Panthers at a radical chic gathering in Hollywood: "He was no Black Panther," Gary writes. "He wasn't even a white panther. The general impression was of a pet poodle pissing on the carpet."[5]

Beyond my premature question (why not write about it?), which was not yet Arafat's, there is in Genet's book a remarkable statement about the Panthers that has the merit of looking not merely forward to the Palestinian episode but backward to Genet's novelistic *oeuvre*. For the moment I shall merely quote it: "For any revolutionary movement," he says, "what are needed are moments of looting and plunder, bordering on fascism, lapsing into it on occasion, surfacing again and then plunging back in with even greater intoxication" (424). Genet's Panthers, that is, represented a protracted flirtation with fascism. And they represented, according to the author, not only a dry run for the Palestinians he would come to cherish but, I would add, a harking back to the poetry of evil of, say, his *Pompes funèbres*.

That link between the humanitarian spokesman for all the *damnés de la terre*, as Juan Goytisolo called him, and specifically the Palestinians, on the one hand, and the self-described poet of evil that has so fascinated and inspired the likes of Sartre in *Saint Genet* and Derrida in *Glas*, on the other, between the apologist, on aesthetic grounds, for the World War II massacre at Oradour (in *Pompes funèbres*) and the denouncer of the massacre of the Palestinians at Chatila in 1982, is the subject of the remarkable centerpiece of Eric Marty's book, *Bref séjour à Jérusalem*, published in Philippe Sollers's collection *L'Infini* in 2003.[6] In that extended essay, first published in *Les Temps modernes*, Marty poses the question of whether one has the right to read the whole of Genet's work from the perspective of "the question of his anti-semitism."[7] And specifically of the anti-Semitism of his last Palestinian period. Marty, that is, is far from Sartre's flip dismissal of what he knew to be Genet's anti-Semitism (according to which, since Genet claimed he could not bring himself to sleep with a Jew, "Israel would be able to sleep tight"). The implication is that something crucial is being played out in the apparently marginal issue of Genet's alleged anti-Semitism, and one measure of its centrality is the question of how one is to view, say, Derrida in his masterwork, *Glas*, a book not only crucially concerned with Genet, but one in which Derrida pretends to discover his own Judaism in the text of *Notre Dame des Fleurs* (the taboo tattoos on the bodies of the penitentiary inmates or *colons* compared to the sacred inscriptions forming the *colonnes* of the Torah, the gender flip between *colons* and *colonnes*, etc.).

"Vingt ans après" is the title of Claude Lanzmann's preface to the initial publication of Marty's chapter on Genet.[8] Twenty years after the massacres of Chatila and Sabra, of course, but I couldn't help thinking of a second, more personal resonance of the title. Twenty years earlier I had published in the same Infini series a volume on the legacies of prewar anti-Semitism in postwar France, a work centered on a reading of Blanchot, and specifically on the repercussions of the anti-Jewish texts, including a call to terrorism, Blanchot had published in the 1930s at the inception of his career.[9] My question, that is, had been precisely symmetrical with Marty's: not what if one were to read Genet from the perspective of the anti-Semitism of late Genet, but what if one were to read Blanchot from the perspective of the anti-Semitism of early Blanchot? All the while keeping alive a sense of the central importance of each *oeuvre.* Blanchot for me, and Genet, who, according to Marty, alone kept alive the hope that French literature might be "something other than the stale ceremonial of a church in the process of being abandoned."[10] And just as Derrida, in *Glas,* would claim to rediscover his Judaism in a (compromised) Genet, French thought—and preeminently Derrida, it could reasonably be claimed—had discovered its own philo-Semitism in a (compromised) Blanchot. Thus there was between Marty's Infini volume of 2003 and my own of twenty years earlier a curious symmetry, as though one aspired to be for the age of what Taguieff has called the "new Judeophobia" what the other had aspired, successfully or not, to be for a more classic phase of the Vichy syndrome.

But what of Genet's alleged anti-Semitism? Let me proceed, drawing in part on Marty, on two fronts: one in terms of statements about Jews, the other, more interestingly, in terms of structure. No need, it will be said, to confuse a rigorously anti-Zionist stance with anti-Semitism. But Genet is too honest, too politically incorrect, for that. He does not shrink before a key question: "Had it not been waged against the people striking me as the most shady, . . . pretending to and wanting to remain the Origin, the people calling itself the obscure night of time itself, would the Palestinian revolution have attracted me so forcefully?" (239). To have asked the question, Genet suggests, is already to have answered it. The Jews, who represent the origin, the ethical good, ethics as origin, are precisely what imbues their enemy, the Palestinians, with their particular chic—*le chic feddai*—or sexiness. For make no mistake: the Palestinian cause is not a matter of justice, but of *justesse,* a dimension both aesthetic and erotic: "I had welcomed their revolt in the same way that a musical ear recognizes the right note—*la note juste*" (17). And further on: "It's not the justice of the cause but its *justesse* that will have touched me" (582). It is the aesthetic, counterpoised against the ethical, that accounts for the numerous musical references—from the Mozart Requiem to Palest(r)ina to a Beyrouth Opera behind which one wants to read "Bayreuth"—in the text. But the aesthetic, in Genet's gay wisdom, is compounded by the erotic. The preference for *justesse* over *justice* in *Un captif amoureux* finds a precise counterpart in "Quatre heures à Chatila": "They [the Palestinians] have right on their side since I love them."[11] And how, finally, is one to distinguish between the aesthetic and the erotic when it comes to the Palestinians? The "beauty" of their "amused insolence" bespeaks a "sensual joy so strong that it wants to drive out all eroticism."[12] As for the Jews, they are left with nothing but the bankruptcy of their ethical imperatives, a fatigue that brings them to want to escape their millennial burden by wallowing in the guilt Genet would assign them for the massacre, performed by a Christian militia with the alleged go-ahead of Ariel Sharon, at Chatila: "The inquisitorial and vengeful saint, Israel, had allowed herself to be judged without sentiment."[13]

Such is the substance of Genet's Nietzschean anti-Judaism: the Palestinians are Mozartian, creatures of a "spectacular pantomime" that at one point has the author invoking *A Midsummer Night's Dream*.[14] The Jews are the incarnation of "Judaic morality," protagonists in a "metaphysical struggle" against a series of "live rebellions" that happen only contingently to be embodied by the Palestinians (543). Yet for all the amoralism of Genet's stance, both the structure of *Un captif amoureux* and the impetus of "Quatre heures à Chatila"—Genet's attempt, as Marty calls it, to write a prose *Guernica* for the second half of the twentieth century—are highly moralistic and even sentimental.

Consider first the structure of the longer work. The armature of Genet's last work entails a search for time past. Specifically, Genet, who had known the "spectacular pantomime" or *féerie* of life in a Palestinian camp in Jordan in 1970, and who was particularly taken with the couple formed by Hamza, a young fedayee, and his mother, decides, in 1984, to return, two years after the slaughter in Chatila, to seek out the cherished pair. The mother-son couple itself is occasionally compared to a pietà statue, at others characterized in terms of incest. The key point is that the redemption of a lost "féerie" and the time elapsed since then in terms of recovering a lost mother-son intimacy is as Proustian a configuration as may be imagined. Add to the mix the fact that Genet is served tea by the mother at a crucial juncture and that things begin to take on clarity, as in the courtyard of the Guermantes hotel, "by way of the specific slope of the ground, the angle my soles formed with the terrain," and the Proustian intertext is reinforced. But matters are clinched when Genet's entry into the Palestinian mother's house is the occasion of an experience of what Marty calls "involuntary reminiscence,"[15] which might just as well have been called "involuntary memory": "I don't know in what manner that Palestinian house, in the Irbid camp, was simultaneously Germanic. What I am writing is nothing I thought out rationally, but rather experienced abruptly, the way one experiences the unripeness of an apple before one picks it, when one detects the green or even before one detects it. The house was not built with materials from the Black Forest, but between it, or rather, between the way it looked and the sound of the word *Allemagne*, Germany, I intuited an affinity that went deeper than I have said; I intuited the affinity that is established when one speaks of Germany and the Grand Mufti of Jerusalem" (571). That is, in the midst of a sentimental visit, apparently to proclaim solidarity with the "wretched of the earth," the aesthetic resurfaces in the form of an "accord," a chord; but what that affinity mediates is the affirmation—in the person of the Grand Mufti, who spent the war years as Hitler's guest in Berlin—of collusion between Palestinians and Nazis.

We have already noted that *Un captif amoureux* marked a return to literature after thirty years of relative sterility. But there had been a second void in Genet's life. Asked by Hubert Fichte in an interview in 1975 whether he had shucked off the maddening admiration for Hitler characterizing *Pompes funèbres*, he replied: "Yes and no. [Hitler's place] was vacated, but the place has not been occupied by anything else; it's empty."[16] That the void of creativity and the void left by Hitler should be simultaneously overcome in an experience of involuntary memory is as sinister a reactivation of the Proustian paradigm as might be envisaged.

We touch here on the question of the twin massacres in Genet's work: Oradour and Chatila. From *Pompes funèbres*: "I am told that the German officer who ordered the carnage at Oradour had a rather gentle face, looked quite sympathetic. He did what he could—a lot—for poetry. He did well by it. . . . I like and respect that officer."[17] Poetry, being complicit with evil, cannot but exult in a Nazi massacre. How then are we to square this with the work of moral witness that "Quatre heures à Chatila" pretends to be? Two answers have been offered. From the Genet camp, Jérôme Hankins suggests that the distinction between the endorsement of Oradour and the condemnation of Chatila bespeaks an awareness of the difference between fantasy and reality: "For at Chatila, reality and History brutally staged and allowed to be seen as objective reality, elsewhere than inside himself, the poet's inner secret charnel house, the mud at the base of his mind from which he had until then been able to mine an inexhaustible supply of images and beautiful sentences."[18] To which one wants to object: Have we come so far with Genet simply in order to reinstate the distinction between fiction and nonfiction it was his signal accomplishment so artfully to have scrambled? There is, of course, a second, more economical way of reconciling the two propositions: what the endorsement of Hitler (Oradour) and the denunciation of Israel (Chatila, but at a remove) share is a common anti-Semitism.

The point is worth considering in the context of the would-be *Guernica* Genet called "Quatre heures à Chatila." Parisian *doxa*, in the person of Didier Eribon, has recently seen fit, in *Une morale du minoritaire: Variations sur un thème de Jean Genet*, to endow Genet with the status of moral guide.[19] The prototype of Genet's moral wisdom is his treatment of the Barcelona transvestites called "Carolines" in *Le Journal du voleur*. A dialectic of shame and pride, an "hontologie" of existence, in which the pariah plunges ever deeper into shame in order to better fuel his pride, lies at the heart of Eribon's promotion of a moral Genet, a Genet suited for an age of "queer theory." And Alain Milianti, who has produced a stage version of "Quatre heures à Chatila," claims that the Carolines episode, with its celebration of the unabashed abjection of "Les Filles de la honte," deserves consideration as the tutelary text for understanding Genet's investment in the Palestinians.[20] There would be, in Eribon's words, a "social isotopy of exclusions," "a homology between all pariahs."[21] All of which would be convincing were it not for two egregious cases, which come with their own logic:

1.   From *Un captif amoureux*: "'That much fragility is an aggression that calls for repression.' I probably tell myself as much, but differently, and it may be supposed that I was traversed by images of naked or almost naked Jews, emaciated in the camps, where their weakness was a provocation" (79). Thus the Jews are the case that escapes the logic of the "social isotopy of exclusions."

2.   Perhaps the historical case that best instantiates Genet's dialectic of shame and pride is Pétain's wartime Milice. From *Pompes funèbres*: "I want to say a few words about the admirable solitude accompanying

the members of the Milice in their relations with the French and with their comrades, and finally in death. They excited greater contempt than whores, thieves, witches, pederasts, more than a man who, either inadvertently or by predilection, would have eaten human flesh. They were not only hated they were vomited up. I love them."[22] The prototypal pariah, metamorphosing his shame into a redemptive insolence, turns out to be the collaborationist *milicien*.

Thus once again, as in the case of the differing reactions to two massacres (Oradour and Chatila), what is an anomaly for the "isotopy of social exclusions" may be resolved through an appeal to a very different logic: that of the anti-Semitism of an author the French intelligentsia, in its most official (Eribon) and eminent representatives (Sartre, Derrida, but also Foucault), has been prepared to look to as an ethical guide.

13

Mother Harvard

Before Yale and its turbulence, there was Harvard, here recollected in tranquility in contributions to two anniversary reports . . .

To the Twenty-fifth Anniversary Report (1990)

A graduate of the Harvard that made sure, at least in those days, that if you did well by her she would give you a year to sort things out at leisure abroad, I left Cambridge for Aix-en-Provence on a Fulbright in 1965, and came back a year later with an abiding interest in psychoanalysis and French literature. After five years at Yale—a semester of which was spent reading Ariosto around a small table with Bart Giamatti, whose death yesterday I feel as being as much a milestone as this Twenty-fifth Anniversary—I began a teaching career that has seen me through a couple of years at Cornell and a visitingship at Berkeley, before more prolonged stays at Johns Hopkins and, now, Boston University. In the early years I was one of those intent on (at last!) bringing home to readable English the speculative effervescence then erupting in France under the name of "(post-)structuralism." In retrospect it appears I was sufficiently polemical to alienate a goodly fraction of the old guard of my profession. Since then—during the period in which (post-)structuralism has ridden high in American academia—I have been sufficiently thorny in my delineation of some of *its* blindspots as to have alienated a similar fraction of the new establishment. All in all, writing, though, perhaps even more than teaching, has been a great source of exhilaration.

The other principal source of delight in my life I date to my marriage in 1977 to Alicia (who is Argentine), my then colleague at Hopkins, whose first novel, about to appear in Spanish, has already been translated into English. Natalia was born in 1978 and is as funny as she is bright. Ezra came in 1984, and I'm only now (for his own good) learning how to resist his charms. . . . I occasionally try to bootleg a little French into their lives (although Spanish is of necessity their second language). Natalia's first stab transformed "Sonnez les mâtines" into "Solomon and Tina," and Ezra, deep into Victor Hugo at age four, has become an aficionado of what he calls "The Hunchback of Nutri-Grain." They've been good years, these. Very good.

To the Fortieth Anniversary Report (2005)

Like everything else around, I've become a bit globalized in recent years. Alicia and I have bought and renovated an apartment in Buenos Aires, which we look forward to occupying when we can. I suppose I should mention a very local reality as well: after twenty-five years in Newton, we are moving to Beals Street in Brookline, the block where JFK was born. When I consider that adulthood for most of us began with his death in 1963, and that the first glimmer of old age, for me at least, appears to be beginning a few yards away from his birth, I can't help savoring life's way of repeating itself—in reverse.

Work has been good. As a University Professor at Boston University, I've had the pleasure of coming to know some stellar talents (and to mourn their passing—Saul Bellow's most recently). As to what my books will have amounted to, I found myself the other day listing the various figures I have been compared to, in anger or enthusiasm, over the years: early on, for my contentiousness, to André Breton (in *Encounter*); for my focus on French anti-Semitism, to Stavrogin, one of the "possessed" (in France's *Nouvelle revue française*); for whatever interpretive wit I may have, to Walter Benjamin (in the *TLS*); and for whatever light I may have shed on France in World War II, to the historian Paxton (in the preface to the French translation of my last book). So imagine a floating poker game—did I say globalized?—bringing the four of them together: a Frenchman, a Russian, a German, and an American. It's far from over, it's rather intense, and, at some level, I suspect, it may very well be . . . *me*.

Good luck to us all!

14

The Heart of the Matter:
A Graduation Address

Academic ceremony has generally been more a begetter of cynicism than of wisdom. In the words of the British poet Ted Pauker, who may have penned the ultimate graduation speech: "Good night to the Year Academic / It finally crept to a close: / Dry fact about physic and chemic, / Wet drip about people and prose." Some years ago, however, upon being asked to deliver an address to students in Modern Languages and Literatures, I resisted the temptation of just such cynicism and did my best to clarify the stakes inherent in four years of study.

*

First things first: my warmest congratulations to you all for a job well done. I've called these remarks "the heart of the matter" because after years of laboring in the vineyards of Babel—four for the undergrads, perhaps even more for the graduate students—it seemed to me you deserved nothing less. So, this being commencement, let us ponder first things: How did you, how did we, get into this business of modern foreign languages and literatures in the first place?

Here are three possible answers. The first is a fable told me by a very sage colleague, Benno Varon. It's the story of a cat who chases three mice back into their hole. The mice are relieved to have escaped their tormentor. The cat, though, waits fifteen seconds and emits the following sound: Woof! Woof! The mice, who are smart, reason that the dog has come and chased the cat away. Whereupon they emerge from their hole and are in short order gobbled up by the cat.

Moral of the story: it pays to learn a foreign language. So there's a first potential reason: you got into this field because you thought you could make a killing with it. Well, I'm not sure I'm convincing you, and I suspect I'm convincing your parents even less.

So let's try another, more exalted path. George Steiner tells us that he has always suspected that the biblical story of the Tower of Babel was a cover-up of sorts. God, you see, was not punishing man for his impudence with a proliferation of tongues, but rather blessing him for the idealism embodied in that spiraling skyscraper. And Steiner has a point: even in their confusion there is an irresistible poetry in the multiplicity of languages. Let me give you a personal example. I teach French, but also possess German, which ebbs and flows according to how much reading I do in it. One day, I found myself reading the great Walter Benjamin in German on the city of Naples. In the piazza, there was a vendor hawking something called *Zahnpasta*. What could *that* be? Well, *pasta* in Naples made perfect sense. But *Zahn*? Of course, *Zahn* means tooth, the Yiddish *Zähne*, if you will. So *Zahnpasta* meant *pasta al dente*. Yum. How smart! Guess again: it means toothpaste. Ever since, I've been unable to eat spaghetti without detecting a faint aftertaste of chlorophyll. Now, if you're secure in your German, unaffected by the Babelian confusion of tongues, you would be deprived of the small poetic charge this story may have given you. So here's to George Steiner and his notion of the blessings of Babel. . . .

But surely this is a pleasure that comes late in the day, not at all how one initially got into this field. No, in the beginning, I suspect, was something far more fundamental: an intuition, perhaps philosophical, almost religious, that there was another world, a better world somewhere else, where they ordered things, named things, differently, perhaps better—a world to which one could only aspire. An act of love, then, almost of religious devotion. Let me offer an example from French: The best government we Americans can think of we call democracy. The French, at their most inspired, talk less of democracy than of the republic. The difference? In the words of Régis Debray, who lectured here a couple of years ago: "La démocratie est ce qui reste d'une république quand on a éteint les Lumières." Which means literally that democracy is what remains of a republic once one has turned out the lights. Ah, but the lights, *les Lumières,*

mean Enlightenment as well, that special eighteenth-century ideal of reason and excellence, excellence through reason. So democracy, majority
rule, is all that's left once the population has lost that commitment to ra-
tional excellence which, one is led to believe, is the special province of
France and its Republic. One can fall in love with such a notion, as one
can, more irrationally, with the bouquet of a wine, the lilt of an accent,
or the shadow cast by a wall on a cobblestone street. And one can devote
a life—or at least four years—to investigating or deepening that mystery.

It is a beautiful notion, but in many ways an illusion. As if to tell
you that your ideal other world has little use for your notion of it, the
world at large seems hell-bent on learning English—because that's where
the money is. And a thirst for money—which I don't for an instant want
to denigrate—will be the world's answer, more often than not, to your
idealism.

Some of you may have seen a wonderful film called *Breaking Away*.
It's about a midwestern kid with a wild, almost irrational, passion for Italy,
which he indulges by listening to, indeed bellowing out, Italian arias, but
also by learning how to ride a sleek Italian bike faster than anyone in the
state. And then the big day comes: the international bicycle race with a full
contingent of bona fide Italian competitors. He is in awe—how wouldn't
he be?—until the race begins and he becomes aware that the Italians—his
beloved Italians!—are illegally colluding to trip him up, lock his wheels,
and force him out of the race. How he negotiates that disillusionment is a
lesson in character, and I offer this crisscross of affections as a cautionary
tale about the difficulties of sustaining genuinely noble sentiments in an
occasionally ignoble world.

So the world is returning your affection for its languages by rush-
ing to English and the cash benefits it is expected to yield. Soon you, who
love Paris, will go to France, and looking down at your money will no longer see the faces of Victor Hugo, Debussy, or even Saint-Exupéry's Little
Prince smiling back at you. On the new Euro, there will be an open window (opening on to nowhere in particular) on one side, and a generic
bridge on the other. As Europe becomes the world's largest market, as the
land of your dreams becomes a division of a supermarket, you will be chal-
lenged in your faith. It may be difficult, amidst the crisscross that can feel
like a double cross, to remain true to the disinterested love that brought
you here. I trust, though, that you will.

You are also the trustees of another legacy that may be equally threatened. Remember the scene in *The Hunchback of Notre-Dame* when Claude Frollo waves a book in front of the cathedral and says: "Ceci tuera cela" (This—book—will kill that—that cathedral). With the advent of movable type, the time of cathedrals as repositories of a culture's wisdom had waned. And how many, in a culture awash in electronic images, have more or less waved a DVD over a book and felt inclined to say, "Ceci tuera cela"? This is not the time to lament the loss of inwardness which the general decline in literacy and in the rhythms of thought it fosters seems to have occasioned. Irony, says Kundera, is the distinctive medium of the novel; but cynicism is that of the couch potato. Keep changing the channels—but never turn the set off. In Cambridge, England, the anthropologist Clifford Geertz ran a symposium titled "Literacy Is Doomed." To the stupefaction of Mario Vargas Llosa, it proved to be a depressingly upbeat occasion. The videosphere, to use the jargon of Régis Debray, seems to be decisively displacing the graphosphere. Our only hope, it has been suggested, may be to stage silent read-ins or book giveaways at video rental outlets.

Reading—serious reading—has been at the center of your studies, and its cultivation is a glorious burden you bear with you as you head into the world at large. It is a threatened legacy. There is a great library on the other side of the river named the Harry Elkins Widener Memorial Library. It was named after one of the victims of the *Titanic*. But at times, reading our cultural pessimists, one has the feeling that the true connection between great libraries and the *Titanic* is that they may be our new *Titanic*s. The art of reading is sinking fast. It is up to you to man the lifeboats.

Let me end, then, with what appears to me to be the world of literature's curious response to the schlock epic film *Titanic*. It is a wonderful novel called *Le Testament français*, translated as *Dreams of My Russian Summers*, and was written in glorious French by a Russian named Andrei Makine. Curiously enough, he could not get it published until he pretended that it had been translated from the Russian. It won the coveted Goncourt Prize a few years ago. (Now *there's* someone who made a killing with a foreign language!)

But what is the connection with the film *Titanic*? The book is the fictional memoir of a Russian brought up in an apartment in Siberia by a loving grandmother. She, in her privileged youth, had, until the Revolution, spent part of every year in Paris, and many years later would take her grandson out onto the balcony overlooking the Siberian plains and wow him with stories of an elegant French world before World War I that was no more. The child fell in love with her stories, which is to say, he fell in love with France, and above all with her tales of the flooding of the Seine in 1910. So much so that every evening as she began her tales of the Belle Epoque, that enchanted era, he would imagine the floodtides rolling in over the Siberian plains and then—miracle—the steeples of Paris emerging, like the peaks of some lost continent, from the water.

A bit like *Titanic*, then, if you remember the film: a glorious world of pre–World War I elegance reclaimed from the depths. But what of the principal difference? The achievement of *Titanic*, you'll recall, was largely one of special effects: the ship goes down virtually in real time. And that still is the mystery of the sinking of the *Titanic* for most of us: it was an event at once so sudden—a crash—and so slow; the agony lasted for hours. And at the end of the film one emerges, dazed by all the water pouring in at one and by all the money, one keeps thinking, pouring into the special effects. Not so the book I'm talking about. The horrendous counterweight to the nostalgic pleasures of pre–World War I elegance—France in the book, the luxury liner in the film—is not the whoosh of water and money, but a finely etched evocation of the nightmare of Leninist, then Stalinist Russia as it severs that special link to Gallic delights which no future Russian generation would ever again savor.

It is as though the graphosphere, the world of print, in what some have regarded its twilight, were throwing up a final supreme challenge to the videosphere about to engulf and supplant it.

So my final advice is not much more profound than that which you may have gotten from your high school teachers. Search out the best, most demanding books you can find; think for a moment of Machiavelli donning his ceremonial raiments in order to read; dress yourself up however you like; but by God, there's much hanging in the balance, take those books and read them.

SEMBLABLES ET FRÈRES

15

Louis Wolfson

However distressed a number of the Yale French faculty may occasionally have been by the single-mindedness of my fidelity to the analyses of Charles Mauron, there was one member of the faculty who could perceive the interest of what I was up to. He was Tzvetan Todorov, visiting at Yale for the academic year 1967–68 and then at the beginning of his distinguished career. (I well remember the first session of his course, which I sat in on. Todorov, whom I had never seen before, had arrived early and taken a seat in the classroom. When I first saw him, his manner a curious combination of angularity and gentleness, copious of hair but in a distinctly European way, I thought here was precisely the kind of cool cat whom one might expect to find in a class taught by the man alleged to be at the forefront of the "structuralist" vanguard in literary studies.) Todorov and I became friends during that year and above all during the following year, when I had the good fortune to be the Yale exchange fellow at the Ecole normale supérieure and he was living nearby in the square Adanson. (At the time there were only two American fellows annually at the prestigious Ecole, one from Yale, the other from Harvard. The numbers have swelled since then, in what sometimes strikes me as the French equivalent of renting out the Lincoln Bedroom.) It turned out that he and I shared the same birthday, which we celebrated that year together.

The turns in Todorov's career are themselves a subject of fascination. I remember reading a book he wrote at a turning point in his thinking, *Critique de la critique,* and being irresistibly reminded of the plot of the

Robin Williams film *Moscow on the Hudson*: a star performer in the Russian (formalist) circus comes to Paris and, to the astonishment of all, defects to the West. It was, he wrote, as though he had been called back to moral seriousness by separate conversations with Isaiah Berlin and Arthur Koestler, two East European giants who had communicated to him that the structural hijinks at which he was so adept were perhaps not a suitable exercise for a talent born in Eastern Europe . . . Todorov's generosity to me over the years has been considerable. There was, in 1969, the invitation to speak at Cerisy at the colloquium on the teaching of literature that he organized with Serge Doubrovsky, and, some years later, an invitation to speak about Blanchot before World War II, a subject on which we communed, at his seminar at the Ecole normale supérieure. On the occasion that interests me in this context, his generosity took the form of an invitation to write a piece on psychoanalysis and literature for *Poétique*, the vanguard journal he was just then founding with Gérard Genette and Hélène Cixous. (And I am reminded that it has been my curious fate to be present at the very beginning or the very end of a number of influential journals: not merely that early issue of *Poétique* but, in the United States, *Diacritics* and *Glyph*, both of which I helped to found and edit; and then, at their demise, the legendary *Tel Quel*, whose two final pages, a letter of errata, bear my signature, and, in this country, the equally legendary *Partisan Review*, for one of whose final issues I wrote an essay on Cynthia Ozick.) I still recall the elation with which I wrote that first essay for *Poétique,* largely while holed up in a first-story café over the place de l'Odéon.

Then there was the happiness of correcting proof, this time (what the hell—I was an American graduate student publishing in *Poétique*! I *earned* it!) at the Deux Magots. I remember strolling into the adjacent bookstore, La Hune, once I had finished my corrections, and stumbling on a book whose title intrigued me: *Le Schizo et les langues ou la phonétique chez le psychotique*, by one Louis Wolfson.[1] It was a bizarre production, all the stranger for having attracted the support, in the way of a preface, of Gilles Deleuze, a thinker who had only recently, like Derrida, pulled off the trifecta of publishing three mind-changing books, works of genuine brilliance, in a single year. As I browsed through Wolfson's book, I managed to piece together, through his ludicrously ungrammatical French, the terms of his argument. The self-described "schizo" was, in fact, a New York Jew whose principal symptom was an inability to bear hearing words of his "mother tongue," English, which he assimilated to morsels of poisoned food with which she, his mother, was attempting to penetrate, stuff, and no doubt annihilate him. Faced with this mortal danger, he had developed a series of defenses, evoked at length in his memoir. The first, plainly uneconomical, consisted in stuffing his fingers in his ears as soon as his mother threatened to "penetrate" him with the most trivial of commonplace questions (e.g., "Can I have a sheet of paper?"). More effective was the use of headphones attached to a transistor radio tuned to one of New York's foreign language stations. Finally, most original of all was a strategy for neutralizing any English he might hear by transforming the words into real or imagined cognates from any one of a series of foreign languages— French, German, Russian, and Hebrew—he had taken to studying with a passion. Now, as I browsed through Wolfson's memoir, I was stunned to recognize, from a series of details, the unnamed New York high school (allegedly for the scientifically gifted!) at which Wolfson had studied. It was the Bronx High School of Science, an exam school, and it was also the high school at which I, thirteen years Wolfson's junior, had studied. So here we were, Wolfson and I, no doubt the only two graduates of the Bronx High School of Science to be publishing, with a certain prominence at that, in French, and he was a certified schizo. Which raised the question: What, precisely, was I? And I thought of the atmosphere of the Yale French Department, in which I was then immersed. Yale, architecturally, was a masterpiece of Depression Gothic, cordoned off by an expanding highway system from a black ghetto, then on the brink of exploding in protest at the apparent injustice of the murder trial of Black Panther leader Bobby Seale. With all the political turmoil of the late sixties in New Haven, I remembered that one of the ongoing anxieties of graduate students in the French Department (but perhaps it was our fantasy) was that Henri Peyre, then teaching at Yale and the doyen of French studies in the United States, would not by *pleased* if he were to hear any of us speaking English in the vicinity of the department in Harkness Hall. Plainly Louis Wolfson, with his Bronx Science diploma, his anxieties about his mother tongue, and his publication in French, was someone I would have to attend to. I bought the book and devoured it.

The result of my reading was an essay I published in an early issue of *Diacritics*, the would-be journal of the critical vanguard which we were then founding at Cornell.[2] I found myself, perhaps in order to avoid addressing

Wolfson's affinities with my own situation, playing him off against a variety of literary characters I was then preoccupied with. There was, a sign of the times, Alexander Portnoy, Roth's early hero, who, in flight from the vulgarity of a shrill and ubiquitous mother, a weak father, had developed a spiel regarding his New Jersey–Jewish name: "Portnoy, yes, it's an old French name, a corruption of *porte noire*, meaning black door or gate. Apparently in the Middle Ages in France the door to our family manor house was painted."[3] (Yes, this was close enough to Wolfson, but also to that petit-bourgeois fantasy of identification with an imaginary aristocracy, the fuel of so much study of France in the United States during its heyday.) Not to mention Portnoy's alter ego: suicidal Ronald Nimkin, a dutiful son and "walking zombie." That persona of the virtuous creep served as a transition, in my essay, which I called "Portnoy in Paris," to the character of the Self-Taught Man in Sartre's *La Nausée*. For it was difficult to think of Louis Wolfson, with his permanent station in the slightly louche Main Reading Room of the New York Public Library on Forty-second Street, without being reminded of Sartre's own zombie of a self-styled "humanist," spending his days at the public library of Bouville. And just as the Self-Taught Man had a spurious fantasy of completeness (since his will to encyclopedic knowledge marked the final degeneration of the Enlightenment dream), so Wolfson dreamed of composing a universal language: the language he would construct, in his neutralization of envenomed English, would end up combining *all* languages through the author's system of cognates and their transformations.

In my essay, I suggested that the fundamental fantasy of Wolfson, to that extent, was to construct the Tower of Babel, a language in which all other languages could commune. Only to the extent that propositions in the new language would be—in sound and sense—more or less identical to the English-language sentences they were intent on destroying, this would be a Tower of Babel that is busy dismantling itself even as it is being constructed. (And suddenly it occurs to me that this Tower of Babel falling even as it rises would be repeated, in its way, on the cover of my second book, *Revolution and Repetition*, which features a famous etching of the Napoleonic column of the Place Vendôme being torn down. And that without knowing why, I had wanted as the cover illustration for the original edition of my most recent book, *Emigré New York*, a photo of the hull of the ocean liner *Normandie* being raised from the mud after it had been inadvertently set ablaze while dockside in New York harbor, then flooded and capsized, by the Americans intent on turning it into a troop transport ship during World War II. The angle of the hull of the ship being raised from the silt is exactly that of the Vendôme column as it is being lowered with ropes and explosives on the cover of *Revolution and Repetition*. And what if column descending and ship rising were but versions of the self-consuming Tower of Babel I had evoked in "Portnoy in Paris"?)

The closest I came in that essay to indicating the connection of Wolfson's plight with my own was in a critique of Deleuze's spirited introduction. For it seemed clear to me (such was my experience of the Depression Gothic enclave cordoned off from the ghetto at Yale) that the interest of Wolfson's memoir lay not at all in any "antipsychiatric" appreciation of the profound "humanity" of his madness, but in a delineation of the incipient madness of our humanities. Deleuze, in sum, was in full flight from his parapsychoanalytic accomplishment in *La Logique du sens* and en route to the new antipsychoanalytic dispensation he would, in a few short years, call *schizoanalyse*. As an ironic reference to "la fameuse forclusion lacanienne" in the preface to Wolfson makes clear.

Concerning that transition—ultimately out of structuralism—in Deleuze, another episode may shed some light. Shortly after I found myself attending to Louis Wolfson's memoir, I was editing a special edition of *Yale French Studies* titled "French Freud: Structural Studies in Psychoanalysis." Among other pieces, the issue contained my translation of (and introduction to) Lacan's "Seminar on the 'Purloined Letter.'" During a summer stay in Paris (I was teaching at Cornell at the time), I contacted Jacques Lacan to see how he might react to the translation. We met, he sounded me out, and to my distress he insisted on knowing more about the other entries in the issue. (My distress was a function of Lacan's rumored irascibility. At the mention of Laplanche and Leclaire's celebrated article on "L'Inconscient," I could sense his anger rising. I attempted to assuage him, insisting on the pedagogical interest of what they had accomplished. I still remember the rage with which he told me, just before slamming his door in my face: "Believe me, from the pedagogical point of view, one could have done much better!")

In addition, he absolutely insisted on seeing the general introduction to the issue (and an essay I had written on the "floating signifier") before we proceeded any further. This was a matter of some concern since I did not have any copies of the requested materials with me in Paris. I called a friend in Ithaca, Roberto González Echevarría, whom I had given copies of my essays, and requested that he send them to me in Paris as soon as possible. They arrived, I delivered them to Lacan on the rue de Lille, and he instructed me to call him back at a specific time that very evening. When I did so, he immediately requested that I call him back a bit later at another very specific time. As I wandered around Paris, from public telephone to public telephone, Lacan managed to repeat his postponements several more times. The last call received no answer at all.

I confess that I was relieved. The marathon series of calls to the rue de Lille took place on a Friday. That Monday I was scheduled to return to America. Mercifully, there would be no more contretemps with Dr. Lacan. That Saturday morning, I was awakened early in my very modest hotel on the rue Cujas. Since there had frequently been shouting in the hallway throughout my stay, much of it in Arabic, this was not unusual, but I was grateful to be able to take a pensive stroll in what continues to be my favorite place on the planet, the Jardin du Luxembourg. When I returned, it was to see the attendant at the desk in a state of such visible distress that I quickly jumped to the conclusion that there had been a murder in the hotel. There had been a fury in the shouts I had heard all week long that led me to fear a major act of violence in the offing. I was wrong. The clerk, his hands trembling, was whimpering: "Ah! Monsieur, ce docteur Lacan, I can't stand his *voice*. He told me: *What*! He's not *there*! He tells me to call him back and he's not *there*! But this is *obscene*!"

Lacan had called and plainly traumatized the unwitting employee. I immediately called back, but again there was no answer. In short order, however, a *pneumatique* arrived from the master, informing me that he had read my pages only the previous night—"et même tard dans la nuit." He then suggested that if I would stay through Monday (thereby missing my flight) he would do "*tout*—everything—in order to see me" following his return from the country. The message was followed by a postscript containing his phone number in the country with the request that I not divulge it to anyone. A friend was quicker to size up the situation than I was. As she put it: "It's a love letter. You've got to make him suffer." I called up Lacan, who seemed happy to hear my voice and asked whether I would put off my departure for a day. When I answered in the negative, he asked whether I might come by car to visit him at Guitrancourt. Again, I feared I could not oblige him. Whereupon he announced that he would return early to Paris the following day, ordering me to be at my hotel at 8 p.m. to receive his call.

I spent the afternoon packing my bags, while anticipating dinner with Lacan. There was, however, no phone call at 8 p.m., nor at 8:15, nor at 8:30. Lacan, I decided, was taking his revenge on an admirer insufficiently responsive to his wishes. When the call finally came, shortly before ten o'clock, Lacan's voice radiated enthusiasm: "Cher!" he addressed me. "Would you like to dine this evening chez Coconas, place des Vosges?" "Très bien, avec plaisir, docteur, but at what time?" "Why, at eight o'clock, of course, as planned." "But it is already almost ten." His response was not long in coming: "Qu'est-ce que c'est que cette histoire??!! What are you talking about? Go there immediately!" And he hung up.

We were three at the restaurant, perhaps four. The guest I can recall was a Belgian linguist, affiliated with the "Groupe MU," then enjoying a certain prominence. Lacan, being Lacan, caused a bit of a stir. When the glorious whole fish arrived at our table, he immediately—and audibly—declared it the most repulsive thing he had ever seen. When the waiter then offered to remove its head, he replied: "Ne manquait plus que cela! That's all that was missing!" I myself was a bit overwhelmed, obsequiously embroidering from the master's *oeuvre* around whatever statement he might make. It was a bit as though I were receiving his every remark as the theme of an essay question, preceded by the instructions: "Comment, using specific examples, on the following statement." Lacan, in his way, seemed charmed. He turned to the linguist and said: "Qu'est-ce qu'il peut être gentille! Et on dit tant de mal des Américains . . ." (It was not until a year or so later, at a memorable lunch chez Lacan on the rue de Lille, that the Gaullist component of Lacan's notorious bias against the Americans was driven home to me. After he had left the table to see a patient, his wife regaled me with the story of all it took for the two of them, accompanied by Jacques Prévert, to gain entrance to Notre-Dame for the Liberation mass. As snipers began shooting from various recesses of the cathedral, Prévert ducked into a confessional, shouting: "I don't want to die in a church!" Others ducked among the pews; only two figures in the entire cathedral could be observed standing: de Gaulle and Lacan.)

I recall asking Lacan, at that first dinner chez Coconas, what his thoughts were on *Anti-Oedipe*, the volume by Deleuze and Guattari then causing a stir. He looked at me, paused, sighed deeply, and muttered: "I'm

going to tell you something that you are not going to understand." This
time it was my turn. "Qu'est-ce qu'il peut être gentille," I opined to the
Belgian linguist. "Et on dit tant de mal du docteur Lacan . . ." What he told
me was that everything he had to say about *Anti-Oedipe* was to be found
in his seminar on Dr. Schreber. This was entirely coherent. If one was psy-
chotic for having "foreclosed" the structural (or Oedipal) signifier—and
such was the predicament of Dr. Schreber—then it was but a short step to
the proposition that one would have to be mad not to be a structuralist.
Such, I suspect, was the message imparted to me as a challenge by Lacan
(since the taunt that I was not about to understand what he was saying was
received as a challenge), and such no doubt accounts for a measure of the
arrogance—or, more generously, the self-assuredness—of my early writing.
The essay on Wolfson, with its insistence on the "madness" of our (pre- if
not antistructuralist) humanities, may well have derived its tone, if not its
substance, from Lacan's taunt that evening chez *Coconas*.

*

   I met Louis Wolfson in 1975. The occasion was the remarkable colloquium on "schizo-culture" organized by Sylvère Lotringer, the gadfly
professor of French at Columbia University. Inspired by the success of
Anti-Oedipe, Lotringer had managed to assemble an extraordinary array
of countercultural talent from both sides of the Atlantic: Michel Foucault,
Gilles Deleuze, Félix Guattari, R. D. Laing, and John Cage, among others.
Lotringer, who had founded the journal *Semio-text(e)* with the aim of
bringing the effervescence of "French theory" to America on terms less aca-
demically *convenient* than, say, *Diacritics*, the journal I was then involved in
editing at Cornell, had made good on his promise with the "schizo-culture"
colloquium. There were crowds, vociferous street people, reciprocal insults
and accusations of working for the CIA, all of it sufficient to bring about
Lotringer's estrangement, or so it seemed, from his staid colleagues at the
Ivy League institution, where he continues to teach and, above all, to pursue a vanguard publishing series whose repercussions have perhaps been
greatest in the New York art world. (Years later I would meet Lotringer
again, when I was serving on a committee evaluating the Columbia French
Department. My recollection is that our visit to his high-ceilinged office,
its shelves piled high with the slim volumes—"hard and portable, compact
and cost-effective"—he had been publishing for *Semiotext(e)*, was like a

trip to the candy store, with Lotringer inviting the committee members to have their fill of free copies of Baudrillard, Virilio, et al.)

With its affirmation of the liberatory potential of schizophrenia (and a contingent from the psychiatric wards of Bellevue in the audience), the scene was understandably raucous. I was happy to see Félix Guattari, whom I had met the previous year at Berkeley, but sensed that he was not altogether happy to see me, a circumstance requiring some explanation. One morning, in the fall of 1974, I was awakened from my slumbers high on Russian Hill, in San Francisco, and informed by the French consulate that Félix Guattari was in town to speak to a local group of therapists on the subject "Et pourquoi pas une pragmatique transformationnelle et générative?" To its considerable discomfort, the consulate had just ascertained that the visiting lecturer's command of English was by no means commensurate with what had been claimed in Paris to the officials paying for his junket. My colleagues at Berkeley informed the consulate that I was the man who might resolve their dilemma, and so I rushed over to the scheduled presentation to perform simultaneous translation. Or almost. Guattari would make a statement and I would translate. Only, because I was able to gauge the limits of my audience's grasp of what was being said, I would frequently append a brief commentary to my translation. Guattari was plainly less than happy at his sense that the translation was taking about fifteen percent more time than the original and, it seemed to me, openly displeased at the fact that the translated version frequently ended with an amused chuckle from the audience. All of which may explain his limited delight at seeing me at the "schizo-culture" colloquium.

Now, it happened that one of the numerous sources of turmoil at the New York colloquium was Michel Foucault's translator, Mark S***. Caught up in the transgressive headiness of the event, he made a point of inflecting Foucault's characteristically elegant French in as obscene a direction as English would (or would not) allow. The audience could tell something was amiss and began to rebel. Guattari, who knew virtually no English, nonetheless realized there was a problem and began to worry that his own presentation, slated to be translated by the same Mark S***, might run into similar problems. On the other hand, he recalled that the occasion at which I had officiated in San Francisco, despite (or perhaps because) of the chuckles with which it was punctuated, was relatively successful. He consequently asked whether I would translate for his talk. I agreed.

When Mark S***, already frustrated by the audience's impatience with his inflection of Foucault, learned of Guattari's decision, he was furious. Guattari, who was a personal friend of his, relented and decided that we would alternate as translators of his presentation: the speaker, in sum, would be flanked by two interpreters. I was a bit taken aback when the speaker pulled out his text and I could see that he had before him a sheaf of blank pages. He proceeded to intone: "I have the impression that here in the context of Columbia University, I could speak about absolutely anything—how I live, how I work, how I screw (*comment je baise*) . . ." At this point I couldn't resist the symmetry of the occasion and translated "comment je baise," with a wink to the bilinguals in the audience, as "how I make love." That bit of seemliness seemed too much for my fellow translator, who proceeded to grab the microphone from me and to say: "It's disgusting, Félix, he's turning you into a laughingstock: il se fout de ta gueule." Guattari had no idea what was going on, but I had sufficient confidence in the limited patience of the raucous audience with my fellow translator, who had squandered the sympathy of those present with tendentious versions of Foucault. In short order they forced him to return the microphone to me.

I had come up to New York from Baltimore, where I was then teaching (and would be joined at Columbia by my colleague at Johns Hopkins and soon-to-be-wife, Alicia Borinsky, the "schizo-culture" colloquium being one of the more memorably odd moments in our courtship). Now, no sooner had I arrived on the premises than I was collared by Sylvère Lotringer, who told me that Louis Wolfson was present and had a long text, which he refused to read to the public. Might I, he asked, choose a suitable fragment and read it in his stead? The appropriate answer came easily to my lips: if one had learned anything from Michel Foucault, already on the premises, it was that people like myself did not have the right to speak for people like Wolfson. Yes, I would be willing to introduce Wolfson, but no more. Whereupon, Lotringer, who expected as much, interrupted me with the words: "Let me introduce you to Louis Wolfson."

To my horror, he proceeded to do so, with the words: "This is J. M., who has worked on you." Wolfson had his headphones plugged in and seemed remarkably rigid. We exchanged a few words, I wanting to let him know that I was an alumnus of the same high school, he seeming above all interested in news I might have about the commercial success of his memoir. The rigidity of his demeanor convinced me that he was not about to engage in a public reading, and so I complied with Lotringer's request. I still remember the artfully inarticulate sounds emitted by John Cage from the stage as I ruffled through the rather moving pages of the Wolfson text titled "Point final pour une planète infernale! Boum!" As it happened, I was seated in the audience next to the critic Michael Riffaterre. I commented to him that I was still enough of a Foucaultian to want to get up on the stage and simply introduce the speaker, but that having met him and taken the measure of his discomfort, his strange rigidity, I was afraid that if I did so, he might take out a revolver and shoot me. Riffaterre at that point replied sublimely: "Not to worry. So long as he's aiming, you have nothing to fear."

*

It was not long thereafter that I received a letter from a psychiatric nurse, claiming that one of her charges was the mother of Louis Wolfson, and that one of *her* obsessive themes was that her son had been the subject of an article by a professor at Cornell University. At this point in her treatment (she was already dying of cancer), it was important that I send the nurse a copy of the article. Would I do so? I did.

*

In 1992, it was my pleasure to speak at a colloquium in Montreal devoted to the seminal work of Jean Laplanche. Laplanche was then entering a new phase of his work, centered on the centrality to psychoanalysis of a new understanding of the "seduction theory," which Freud, in the classic accounts of the discipline, was said to have abandoned in 1897. That expanded sense of the seduction theory—understood in terms of the unwitting sexual agendas which adults bring to the gratification of infantile needs and the difficulty of children in negotiating them—had already been present in *Vie et mort en psychanalyse*, the volume I had translated and that has always been for me a touchstone of readerly seriousness. But now Laplanche was relinquishing much of the gossamer fabric of his earlier analysis in order to anchor things firmly in the newly generalized understanding of the seduction theory. It was, I thought, as though he were repeating in his own work the gesture he had so deftly analyzed, in the earlier volume, in the work of Freud: losing contact with the most potently attractive aspects of his own thought out of a desire to consolidate them.

My contribution bore a title out of Goethe's *Faust*, "Verweile doch!" and was a plea not to rush to the liquidation of the concept of *Anlehnung* or *étayage*, a kind of "propping" of drive on instinct, that played an extraordinarily suggestive role in the earlier volume.

It was to my hotel room in Montreal, which I was sharing with my wife (she of the "schizo-culture" colloquium) and two young children, that the phone call came. The speaker identified himself in schoolboy French as Louis Wolfson and insisted he wanted to meet with me. I immediately began searching my memory for lost friends from my Cornell days, twenty years before, who might remember my article and think this kind of prank call in any way a joke. And then the speaker explained that he had moved from New York to Montreal "pour des raisons économiques," and things began to fall into place. Wolfson had seen the name of Laplanche on the announcement for the colloquium and assumed that Pontalis, who had, of course, collaborated with Laplanche on the classic *Vocabulaire de la psychanalyse*, could not be far behind. His interest in Pontalis was quite simple. That celebrated analyst had been the director of the series Connaissance de l'Inconscient, which had published *Le Schizo et les langues* at Gallimard, and there was the delicate matter of accumulated royalties that Wolfson was eager to discuss. He soon discovered that Pontalis, however, had not come to Montreal and that I was the only one on hand who knew him. Whence the phone call.

Not without trepidation on my part, we agreed to meet. I had, after all, dined out a sufficient number of times over the years on Riffaterre's sublime rejoinder for it not to be unreasonable for me to fear that Wolfson might be interested in proving him wrong. The meeting would be in front of my hotel, a very public space. I was accompanied by the burliest analyst I could find at the colloquium. My wife and children would be in eyeshot in the lobby. My nervous wait for our . . . reunion, which saw me peering left and right in anticipation, was interrupted by a tap on my back. It was Louis Wolfson himself. I instinctively stretched out a hand, more to reassure myself than him, but my hand was firmly refused. Physical contact was an issue. We exchanged a few words; he expressed disappointment at the absence of Pontalis, almost as though there were something faintly dishonorable about it. And then he retreated back into the city, leaving me to wonder, as I still occasionally do, how many years will elapse before my next encounter with this doppelgänger—but I have agreed to speak in Paris about Pontalis next spring, and maybe that is why—falls due.[4]

16

Walter Benjamin

There were, to begin with, the flashes of coincidence, with their attendant aches. For Benjamin to have given the title *Zentralpark* to a folder
of fragments devoted to Baudelaire meant, it seemed clear to me, that they
were intended as a collection of problems to be elucidated, if not solved,
while strolling through Central Park. (And suddenly the Manhattan park
where I whiled away many an afternoon during my childhood seemed as
though haunted by the ghost of the thinker who never made it to these
shores. Those faintly foreign gentlemen with their courtliness, Borsalino
hats, long overcoats, rimless glasses . . .) Then there was the last letter of
the published correspondence. (But why—first Virginia Woolf, now Benjamin—this fixation on last letters? It is as though the split between *eskaton*
and *telos*, the end as a random cutting short and the end as a concluding
fulfillment, were never better captured than in the experience of reading,
at the end of a collected correspondence, the message whose very random-
ness makes it the furthest thing imaginable from a last will and testament
. . .) On August 2, 1940, not many weeks before his suicide at the Spanish
border, Benjamin wrote to Adorno from Lourdes. Amidst all the signs of
his collapsing situation—indeed, of the collapse, as he put it, of "bourgeois
civilization"—he mentions a flicker of hope: "In Boston, at 384 Commonwealth Avenue, there lives a Mr. Merrill Moore. Mrs. W. Bryher, the editor
of "Life and Letters Today," has spoken to him about me on several occa-
sions. In all probability he has a sense of the situation and the will to help
change it. I think it may be worth your while to get in touch with him."[1]
The final hope, about to be snuffed out, was to come from Commonwealth

Avenue, just down the street from my office of the past twenty-five years. *Ex Bostoniense salus . . .* (The saving angel, Merrill Moore, turned out to be not unknown to my Boston colleagues: a poet and psychiatrist, a compulsive sonneteer spending his time between sanatorium and sonnetorium, as he put it, an original member of the Fugitive *cenacle,* turned out to be the last hope of our fugitive from the chaos in Europe . . .)

But my identification with Benjamin, such as it was, in fact grew out of a more readerly experience. In the early 1980s I found myself reading with growing pleasure and surprise an early book by Terry Eagleton, titled *Walter Benjamin, or Towards a Revolutionary Criticism.* Like many in America at the time, I had heard more than I *knew* of Benjamin, and thus it was with growing fascination that I read Eagleton's slightly Lacanianized take on the German thinker—with allegory intercepting symbol much as the unconscious intrudes on consciousness. Here plainly was a thinker with whom my affinities seemed greater than I had expected. And then, on page 162, to my surprise, I found a discussion of my book *Revolution and Repetition,* part of which Eagleton summarized with genuine brio:

There is, in other words, always something that escapes comic emplotment: there is always a pure residue of difference that is non-dialectizable. But if this is true of tragedy, it is also paradoxically true of comedy itself. In his book *Revolution and Repetition,* [J. M.] sees the elegant dialectical schema of Marx's *The Eighteenth Brumaire of Louis Bonaparte* as fissured by an uncouth, irrepressible cackle of farce: the farce of Bonaparte himself, the non-representative joker in the dialectical pack, riding to power on the shields of a drunken soldiery. The ruin of the Marxist notion of the state as class-representative, Bonaparte prises a crack in that conceptual architecture through which floods a heterogeneous swarm of lumpen-proletarians, a flood that threatens to swamp Marx's own orderly text under the semiotic excess it lends to his language. "The upshot," [J.M.] comments, "[is] a Marx more profoundly an-archical than Anarchism ever dreamed."[2]

Eagleton would take his distance from my position, eventually arguing that the joke was less on Marx than on the bourgeoisie, which found itself giving up all its political rights (free speech etc.) in order to maintain its economic privileges. His point, that is, was to rein in the disruptive force of Marx's analysis in the *Eighteenth Brumaire* and make of it the perfect illustration of the dialectic. (A quarter of a century before, Sartre had come to a similar conclusion in his unfinished book on Mallarmé: with the bourgeoisie, after the December coup, having given up its right to speak its mind, Mallarmé would turn poetry into the alternately sublime and laborious art of saying *nothing*. . .)[3]

Now, whatever the merits of Eagleton's would-be corrective, nothing in the episode affected me so much as the surprise—more uncanny than narcissistic, I can only hope—of discovering a rather deft summary of my own work in a discussion of the efforts of one of the tragic figures of the intellectual history of the twentieth century. And thus began a lasting effort to limn the affinities between Benjamin's efforts and my own. These would surface explicitly in the conclusion of my *Legacies: Of Anti-Semitism in France*. For in that work, I found myself in search of a new coherence in the *oeuvres* of Blanchot, Lacan, Giraudoux, and Gide, once I attempted to re-center them around apparently marginal and forgotten fragments of anti-Semitic rhetoric. In addition, it became clear to me that my efforts, far from diminishing the literary interest of these stained masters, resulted in an augmentation of the aesthetic pleasure they afforded. Now, the new coherence I undertook to elaborate may have been convincing (or at least convincing enough to merit extended mention on the first page of *Le Monde* when the French translation appeared in 1984), but it left me with an enigma of a personal order: What was I, a Jew, doing in restoring—or, worse yet, constructing—a lost anti-Semitic tradition?

There was, of course, the ready-made answer of "Jewish self-hatred" (and Weininger, the high priest of that affliction, would eventually be the subject of an essay of mine devoted to his subliminal influence on a poem of Apollinaire).[4] And should I choose to sublimate the embarrassment of that affliction into the more "theoretically correct" (because ethnically neutral?) category of primary masochism, I had sufficiently mastered the resonances of Laplanche's reading of *Beyond the Pleasure Principle*, the almost symphonic final movement of his *Vie et mort en psychanalyse*, to be able to wring the necessary effects from that reading. But it was to Benjamin that I turned in that conclusion. And I did so by way of his endlessly intriguing friendship with the great historian of Jewish mysticism, Gershom Scholem.

In "Redemption Through Sin," Scholem, in 1937, outlined the surprising afterlife of the Sabbatian movement.[5] Once the notorious "false Messiah," Sabbatai Sevi, had converted under duress to Islam in 1666, the Jewish hordes who had opted to believe in him were faced with a major dilemma. (An apostate Messiah, as Scholem noted, was even more of a challenge to the faithful than a crucified Messiah, such as the Christians—

and such was their genius—came to accommodate.) The Jewish answer to Sabbatai Sevi's conversion, according to Scholem, was to invent a new theology, according to which, at this stage of the redemptive process, it was the Messiah's obligation to enter into evil in order to defeat it from within. And such would be, as well, the imperative faced by his followers. Soon there would emerge, on these grounds, what Scholem, in a dramatic conversation with Benjamin in 1927, at the Café du Dôme in Montparnasse, called "a full-blown antinomianism" within Judaism. The way to fulfill the sacred Law, it was now ordained within the sect, would be to violate it. But the analysis did not stop there. The sect, with its mystically ordained transgressions, persevered, but after a number of generations all it tended to know of itself was its tendency to violate—that is, not to respect—the laws of the faith. And once sufficient time had passed, the remnants of the sect came up with their own justification for their transgressive behavior: the refusal to obey the traditional strictures was attributed to . . . Enlightenment. Whereby the Jewish Enlightenment, in its putative hostility to mysticism, turns out to be nothing so much, in Scholem's reading, as the relic of a decrepit mystical heresy, Sabbatianism, once that heresy had forgotten its own origins.

The Benjamin who has always interested me is the one who might be in the grips of the history recounted by his friend Scholem. In a memoir of that friendship, "Walter Benjamin and His Angel," the historian of mysticism speaks of the Klee painting of an angel that became talismanic of their friendship, but also of a text by Benjamin dealing with an angel and enigmatically titled "Agesilaus Santander."[6] Its subject is the secret name—Agesilaus Santander—given Benjamin by his parents at birth should he ever be required to "demonstrate" that he was not Jewish. Yet it is also compared to the secret Hebrew name traditionally given by Jews to their children. The name is thus simultaneously Jewish and non-Jewish, and, in Scholem's privileged reading, it turns into an anagram of *Der Angelus Satanas*: The Angel Satan. Here then was an antinomian Benjamin, secretly Jewish/non-Jewish, and to that extent, in Scholem's telling, Satanic. He was, as such, the perfect tutelary figure for my (inevitably Jewish) effort in *Legacies* to rediscover—or restore—an aesthetically rich but lost anti-Semitic tradition. To put the best face on things, I too, a crypto-Sabbatian no longer aware of where his deepest motivations might lie, was in my way attempting to defeat evil from within.

Years later, I wrote a volume on the little-known scripts for children's radio that Benjamin had written in an effort to make ends meet once he had been ejected from the German university system.[7] The set of about thirty rambling *causeries*, which Benjamin was commissioned to deliver on schedule, before an invisible audience, from the perspective of childhood, struck me as coming as close to the transcript of a psychoanalysis of Walter Benjamin as one was ever likely to encounter. Yet what was most striking about that imaginary transcript were the two motifs that Benjamin seemed to return to obsessively in his chats: on the one hand, cases of catastrophe (say, the destruction of Pompeii, the flooding of the Mississippi in 1927, or the Lisbon earthquake of 1755); and, on the other, instances of fraud (in the domains of, say, bootlegging and stamp-collecting, or as practiced by the infamous Cagliostro). Now, my effort in the book was to show that at crucial junctures in the collection of scripts there was a meshing of the two series. But if catastrophe and fraud could be shown to be intricately, albeit probably unintentionally, articulated in the ramblings of the scripts, and if catastrophe was the mark of the advent of the Messiah (or for that matter of revolution) within the ongoing dialogue of Scholem and Benjamin, then the interplay between catastrophe and fraud would point specifically in the direction of the Sabbatian motif of the "false Messiah" whose afterlife I had already charted in the conclusion to *Legacies*.

In "Benjamin and His Angel," Scholem made it clear that the "Luciferian element" made its way into Benjamin's meditations on the Klee painting "not directly from the Jewish tradition, but rather from the occupation with Baudelaire that fascinated him for so many years" (87).[8] But here we return to the circumstance that had led Eagleton to summarize my *Revolution and Repetition* at some length in his volume on the German thinker. Eagleton was of the opinion that I was attending far too seriously to the Marxian references to the rollicking *Lumpenproletariat* in Marx's *Eighteenth Brumaire*. What had intrigued me was that the dialectic of the class struggle (between bourgeoisie and proletariat) had been short-circuited by the sudden rise to the pinnacle of society of the lumpenproletarians of what Marx (after Murger) called *La Bohème*, organized as the cohort of the future Napoléon III. Dialectic, in sum, had come to a sinister standstill with the coup d'état of December 2, 1851. Consider now that in his long essay on the "Paris of the Second Empire in Baudelaire," Benjamin's principal point is the affinity between the poet and the bohemians of Paris. More specifically, Benjamin insists on Baudelaire's affinities with the "putschist" sensibility and aspirations of the lumpen bohemia of the city. The would-be putschist is he who makes short shrift of the necessary and growing awareness of the proletariat in its opposition to the bourgeoisie as he attempts to precipitate matters beyond the very category of awareness. As such he is a figure for a certain violence of the unconscious itself. And the two individuals who incarnate that putschist sensibility, born of the lumpenproletarian *Bohème*, are, for Benjamin, Auguste Blanqui and Louis Bonaparte. On the one hand, Baudelaire was profoundly "marked" by the revolutionary prestige of the recurrently unsuccessful insurrectionist Blanqui.[9] On the other hand, as Benjamin put it in *Zentralpark*, "The sudden attacks, the petty three-penny machinations, the surprising decisions are all part of the *raison d'Etat* of the Second Empire and were characteristic of Napoléon III. They supply the essence of Baudelaire's attitude in his theoretical proclamations" (658–659). Thus Baudelaire, the author with whom Benjamin was centrally concerned, interested him in his twin affinities with the unsuccessful bohemian putschist Blanqui and the successful bohemian (or lumpenproletarian) putschist Louis Bonaparte.

The lumpen side of Baudelaire, in that case, would combine both the prevailing power (Napoléon III) and rebellion against that power (Blanqui), or, in other terms, the law and its transgression. Perhaps this is what led Benjamin to insist in his essay on Baudelaire on the dual aspect of Satan: as both the Father of Evil and the great Victim (525). We touch here, it may be suggested, on the antinomian side of Sabbatianism, the law perpetuated as its own transgression, a poet identifying with both the tyrant (Napoléon III) and the rebel (Blanqui).

This can give us the poem that Benjamin quotes at length, *Le Vin des chiffonniers*:

On voit un chiffonnier qui vient, hochant la tête,
Buttant, et se cognant aux murs comme un poète,
Et, sans prendre souci des mouchards, ses sujets,
Epanche tout son Coeur en glorieux projets. (520)

(One sees a ragpicker go by, shaking his head, stumbling, bumping against the walls like a poet. And, with no thought of the stool pigeons, his subjects, he pours out his heart in grandiose projects.)

The "chiffonnier" or ragpicker is preeminently a lumpenproletarian: "lumpen" in German is translated as *chiffon* or rag. Here the would-be rebel, intoxicated with wine but also with his own virtue, fails to realize that he is preaching revolution to a crew of "mouchards," or police spies, no doubt the only individuals who will listen to him (520). His way of working against authority, that is, is a way of working for authority: there is an antinomianism as "full-blown" in Benjamin's Baudelaire, that is, as in the Jewish mystical trend evoked by Scholem at the Dôme in 1927.

As to what the "putschist" violence delineated by Benjamin in Baudelaire is opposed to, we find an instance in the Lamartine poem the critic quotes in the same essay:

Tout homme avec fierté peut vendre sa sueur!
Je vends ma grappe en fruit comme tu vends ta fleur,
Heureux quand son nectar, sous mon pied qui la foule,
Dans mes tonneaux nombreux en ruisseaux d'ambre coule,
Produisant à son maître, ivre de sa cherté,
Beaucoup d'or pour payer beaucoup de liberté! (533)

(Every man can sell his perspiration with pride! I sell my cluster of grapes as you do your flower, happy when its nectar, crushed beneath my foot, flows with amber, producing for its master, drunk with its price, a considerable amount of gold in payment for a considerable amount of freedom!)

We are again dealing with wine, but the intoxication this time is not the drunkard's, high on his virtue, as he preaches an insurrection whose failure is assured by the public of police spies to whom he preaches. It is that of the landowner, getting high on the price of his grapes, said to be the price of ever-expanding freedom itself, even as the poet expresses himself in a manner that resonates with the trampling of the grapes by a delighted peasantry. Such is the euphoric model of self-expression against which the violence of poetry-as-putsch seems to be directed. That self-satisfied plenitude has a methodological counterpart against which the Baudelairean in Benjamin seems to be directing his attack. It is that of understanding through empathy (*Einfüllung*). The dialectical absorption of the other through an act of identification would be the ultimate target of the putschist violence, with its allergy to mediation, celebrated by Benjamin. What Benjamin appears to be objecting to is a narcissistic identification of the soul with the world it perceives as a series of commodities. "Now this 'empathy' is the very essence of the intoxication to which the *flâneur* abandons himself in the crowd. The poet enjoys the incomparable privilege of being able to be himself and others at will" (558). But there is a cheap and deluded triumphalism in the identificatory (or empathic) gesture itself, since what the empathist identifies with, in his quest for immediate (and immediately satisfying) understanding, according to the *Theses on the Philosophy of History*, is the "victor" himself.[10]

Benjamin's Baudelaire, in sum, appears, at some level, to predicate the violence of a coup d'état or putsch against the plenitude of an attitude of dialectical appropriation or identification. To the extent that this coup is linked to the lumpenproletariat, it appears to be superimposable on the Marxian figure of Louis Bonaparte short-circuiting the *dialectic* of the class struggle as he is hoisted to power by his lumpen cohort of the Société du 10 décembre. However inconvenient for the militant, that is, Benjamin would appear to be affirming, through Baudelaire, precisely what I found myself affirming in my reading of Marx . . .

Now, it happens that in addition to having written about Marx's *Eighteenth Brumaire of Louis Bonaparte*, I had also written about Baudelaire and done so in terms congruent with my reading of Marx. (And it suddenly occurs to me that the title of my piece, "Baudelaire with Freud," all but echoes the poetry-with-psychiatry vocation of Merrill Moore, the hoped-for angel of Commonwealth Avenue.)[11] The violence of the putschist (in Benjamin) became superimposable on the violence of the figure of the dandy (in my take on *Le Spleen de Paris*) as he exercises his growing aggressiveness against a figure of narcissistic exhibitionism (a histrion, prostitute, or beggar).[12] The latter begs for the empathy of the dandy and the Baudelairean move is over and again to cut short that movement of charitable (or lustful or admiring) identification. Consider the exemplary prose poem entitled "La Corde": A painter becomes enthralled with the aesthetic potential of a young urchin whom he employs as a model. Eventually he requests of the boy's parents that their child be allowed to live with him. They agree and the child thereupon serves as his model in a series of increasingly lovely portraits: the painter, that is, expresses himself in the figure of the child. Identificatory empathy becomes the very stuff of his art. In this dialectic of master and servant, however, there is a snag: the servant-model through whom the master expresses himself resents his subservience and begins pilfering sweets. Whereupon the master puts him on notice, only to return one day and find to his horror that the boy has hanged himself from a nail over the doorway. However, the quintessentially Baudelairean moment comes not with the shock of the child's suicide, but with a second shock. The child's mother pays the painter a visit and is comforted by the sight of a remnant of the rope with which the boy had hanged himself, still attached to the nail above the doorway. She asks to keep the tufted remnant, whereupon the painter realizes that her hope is to make some money by putting it up for sale among her morbid neighbors. The identificatory dialectic whereby the painter expressed himself in and as the completeness of the image of an other is cut short by the displacements of a "partial" or "component" object, as the analysts say, caught up in a circuit of exchange.

Assume now that "La Corde" is the exemplary Baudelairean prose poem. With the dialectic cut short by the displacements of a remnant—*corde* or *chiffon*—we are back in the configuration of *Revolution and Repetition*: the dialectic of class struggle is abruptly short-circuited by the unexpected rise of the *lumpen* cohort of Louis Bonaparte. All of which would suggest that Benjamin toward the end was thinking in a region somewhere between my analysis of Marx (with its affirmation of the *putschist* side of Bohemia) and my reading of Baudelaire (with its affirmation of the violence exercised by the dandy against the beggar).

Some years ago I found myself asking the poet Richard Howard, in a discussion of his translations of Baudelaire, whether he did not feel deprived by English's inability to capture Baudelaire's transition from feminine *Espérance* to masculine *Espoir* in the course of one of his poems titled "Spleen." When he pressed me on what lay behind my question, I answered that I had always attached special value to the concluding allegory of "Spleen" (LXXVIII), which has feminine *Angoisse* despotically planting her "black flag" on the inclined skull of masculine *Espoir*. It was an allegory, I suggested, whose full wit could be gauged by hearing it resonate with a key image in "La Chevelure": the poet dreams of deliriously losing himself in the jet-black hair of his mistress, described as a "pavillon de ténèbres tendues." That dark "pavilion" is frequently translated as "flag," so that if one juxtaposes the image under discussion with the allegory just attended to, one ends up with a rather hilarious dialogue: the poet announces to his mistress that he would die for her hair, whereupon, removing her black banner of a wig from her head and planting it on his, she says: "You like it? You can have it." It was at this point that Richard Howard trumped me by summarizing my own point with a line out of Baudelaire: "Tu réclamais le soir; il descend, le voici." It remains to this day my favorite line of verse by Richard Howard. Even as it serves to confirm my reading of the poet. Recall the poem from which it is taken, "Recueillement": As much-desired evening settles over the city, the poet calls on a distinctly maternal allegorical *Douleur* to join him far from the whip of allegorical *Plaisir*, to which much of the city prepares to submit. Let that tenderly intimate tandem of mother and son, seeking refuge from Pleasure's sadistic whip, serve as an emblem of a narcissistic ego resisting the attack of the unconscious drive.

*

My reading of Marx had originally been published in an issue of the French journal *Critique* dedicated to the theme of psychoanalysis "as seen from without."[13] My hope was to find some traction in Marx that would allow me to gain some distance from the heady French-Freudian paradigm which had so overwhelmed me. To that extent, of course, my piece, however exhilarating, was a failure. No reading I had done could be more Freudian in its feel than my *Eighteenth Brumaire of Louis Bonaparte*. Decidedly, it was Freud who seemed to have the drop on Marx, and not the reverse. And the fragments of Benjamin on Baudelaire I have attended to until now, although none were published during Benjamin's lifetime, felt like they were part of the general domain I was exploring. *Mon semblable, mon frère*, indeed. Which is why it was of particular interest to me that the one essay on Baudelaire that Benjamin did regard as complete happens also to sport an elaborate reference to Freud.

At a key juncture of "On Some Motifs in Baudelaire," the essay published by Adorno in the 1939 double issue of the *Zeitschrift für Sozialforschung*, Benjamin invokes Freud. After Bergson and Proust, it is the turn of psychoanalysis to make its contribution to the paradigm Benjamin would construct. The text cited is *Beyond the Pleasure Principle* and culminates in what Benjamin calls a "fundamental formula": since "a single excitation can not simultaneously become conscious and leave a measurable trace in the same system," the "most intense and durable" mnemic residues are "those which have never attained consciousness."[14] And since consciousness per se would not contain any mnemic traces, its role would be to protect the psyche from an excess of stimuli rather than to receive them. This formulation points in two directions. On the one hand, consciousness would function above all as a shock absorber, neutralizing stimuli and "sterilizing" them for poetic experience.[15] On the other hand, the resource of poetic plenitude, allied with the Proustian experience of involuntary memory, would lie with the unconscious. It is an unconscious which, in the course of the essay, will famously take on the aura of tradition and the "cultic."

The reader senses the transition to Benjamin's notorious conclusion about the fundamental Baudelairean experience: "the decline of the aura in an experience of shock."[16] What he or she may not have noticed is how precisely the underpinnings of that conclusion reverse those informing the analysis of Benjamin presented thus far. *My* Benjamin, based on a text unpublished by Benjamin during his lifetime, insisted on the unconscious drive attacking the identificatory empathy-driven impulse of the self-serving historicist. That drive found its emblem in the putschist sensibility of Napoléon III or Blanqui, two figures for whom Baudelaire's affinities were underscored by Benjamin in "The Paris of the Second Empire in Baudelaire." The *discontinuity* of the coup, resonating with the unconscious drive at its most sadistic, would interrupt the rich *continuity* or plenitude of an essentially identificatory (or narcissistic) ego. In the published essay of 1939, however, the *discontinuity* of the shock experience, so many coups inflicted by modernity, marks an assault on the rich though subliminal *continuities* of the "cultic" or tradition-bound unconscious. Whereas the earlier configuration seemed to speak to an unconscious aligned with the Freudian id, the later one speaks to an unconscious closer to an anthropologically grounded take on the superego. Such would be the terms of the chiasmus structuring Benjamin's reflections on Baudelaire. If, that is, my parapsychoanalytic reading of Benjamin, afloat between my earlier readings of Marx and Baudelaire, were correct, it would be precisely when Benjamin succeeds in publishing his reflections on the poet, when he sees fit to invoke Freud as a tutelary presence, that he would get things—precisely—wrong.

But what grounds might I offer for the correctness of my take on Benjamin? After all, the later configuration, relating, not without a touch of the elegiacal, the decline of the aura in the age of mechanical reproduction, has its own attractions. It survives at present in the writings of France's most striking essayist, Régis Debray, on the impoverishment of experience as an ever-expanding realm of communication (between individuals, over distance) continues to exact its toll on a waning realm of transmission (between generations, over time). And the aesthete in me finds it hard to resist that position when argued with the panache of Debray.

My reasons for preferring my take on Benjamin's Baudelaire to its reversal in the version which Benjamin came to publish are both textual and experiential. First, as we have seen, there is the choice between an id-based and a superego-based version of the unconscious. Here I would recall the libidinal roots of the superego, the fact that as a psychical instance it appears to enter into Freud's *oeuvre* as it penetrates into the Rat Man: ecstatically, through the latter's anus.[17] The id, that is, appears to be more originary than the superego. Additionally, there is the alignment of the unconscious as Benjamin speaks of it with the notion of "involuntary memory" in Proust. For from the time of my earliest publications it has always seemed to me that "involuntary memory" functioned in Proust more as something on the order of a screen-memory than as any "royal road to the unconscious." In summary: when one considers that the madeleine episode, emblematic of "involuntary memory," is twinned with the scene of the good-night kiss, which issues in the decisive "decline" of the narrator's will, and that the first episode is talismanic of art at its most redemptive, and the second, of life at its most damning, one perceives that the relation between the two is specular, offering positive and negative versions of the same semantic content, and that this relation is the stuff, not of the symbolic (unconscious) but of the (narcissistic) imaginary. Moreover, if the good-night kiss episode is informed by fantasies of fusion with the mother, the madeleine episode harkens back to the night table of Tante Léonie, a character who resembles nothing so much—in her malingering and her will to dominate all around her—as a feminized parody of the narrator. The relation between madeleine and good-night kiss, in brief, is congruent with that discussed earlier between the *ideal* embodied by the jet-black banner of "La Chevelure" and the *spleen* of the black flag in the poem so named. Finally, there is the famous case of the aura, the fading light with which a waning tradition, putatively that of the unconscious, seems to be imbued. Yet consider how the aura is characterized in Benjamin's essay: "To sense the aura of something is to confer on it the ability to raise its eyes."[18] And elsewhere, Valéry is quoted: "In dreams an equivalence is struck. The things I see see me as much as I see them."[19] The aura, in sum, entails a mirroring of the subject in the object of his or her perception— that is, it is shot through with the specific dynamics of the narcissistic ego.

With "involuntary memory," "aura," and the superego itself having left the register of the repressed to flourish in that of the *refoulant*, or agent of repression, the textual grounds for my skepticism regarding Benjamin's final (and quasi-official) take will be clear. What remains to be considered are the experiential grounds. One of the more interesting passages in Benjamin's Baudelaire essay of 1939 involves gambling, more specifically the affinity between the compulsive gesture of the gambler placing his bets on the table and the similarly constrained efforts of the factory worker on the assembly line. Such would be the prototypes of the "shock experience" inflicted by modernity. What is striking (and suggestive) in Benjamin's formulation is the notion of a domain that undercuts the distinction between work (the assembly line) and play (gambling). For the dismantling of such a binary opposition, especially as mediated by the compulsive gesture of a body part—the hand—construable as capable of being detached from the body and circulating through a fantasmatic circuit, seems far more redolent of the unconscious than of the ego, however "degraded" its experience of "experience" may be.

Plainly, here too Benjamin had gotten things backward. Freud was being invoked to shore up an "auratic" reading of the unconscious, steeped in tradition, which would maintain a distinction, say, between (artisanal) work and the play of leisure, a distinction which we have seen scrambled, according to Benjamin, in (degraded) modern consciousness. I suspect, however, that my sense that gambling, in particular, belonged on the other side of the ledger would not have loomed as forcefully for me were it not for a visit to Las Vegas I made in the mid-1970s. It was a trip I had no particular wish to make. About a year before the birth of our first child, Alicia, my wife (or was she then still my wife-to-be?) and colleague at Johns Hopkins, and I, taking advantage of a seemingly endless summer, decided to make the classic trip cross-country by car. The final destination was to be Berkeley, where I had taught a year or so before, and specifically to the home of my friend Howard Bloch, a vintage Maybeck with shards of light invading dark wood interiors in a manner caught by Alicia in some of her most memorable photos.

Now, it happened that during that trip my parents—my father being more of a committed gambler than I at the time realized—were spending time in Las Vegas and insisted that we make a stopover on the way back. The prospect of Las Vegas was not one that intrigued me. No doubt part of my self-definition at the time had something to do with not having *that* much in common with my loving father—in either work (the store) or play (the Strip). (And suddenly I recall the beginning of an essay on my work by Denis Hollier, who had become my friend at Berkeley, and which began by comparing me to Julien Sorel, who made a point of finding a place to read in a particularly noisy corner of his father's mill, the perfect alibi if his father should call him—inaudibly—to assist in work: yes, that may have been even more on the mark than Denis realized . . .)[20] Las Vegas, with its vulgarity, was, in sum, not to be my cup of tea.

It was at the blackjack table that the fever came over me. Deciding to have a (carefully circumscribed) go at the casino, I soon found myself altogether taken with the game. As I tried to understand what was happening to me, it struck me that money in the unreal arena of Las Vegas was like language in psychoanalysis. Cut off from its utilitarian function, from any relation to production (in the case of money) or communication, Mallarmé's "universel reportage" (in the case of words), each appeared to exist in these specially circumscribed circumstances for the sole purpose of being libidinally recharged. It was as though the classical distinction between Washington and Wall Street, governmental superstructure and market infrastructure, had been superseded by a third term, Las Vegas, in which the love of lucre, beyond anything it might *do* for one, could be reignited in its pure state.

It was, moreover, enough for me to glance around the casino during what I am inclined to call my session for me to see just how lumpen a crowd I had, in Las Vegas, fallen into. The resonances with my reading of Marx in *Revolution and Repetition*, that paean to the lumpenproletariat, were overwhelming. It was an odd moment, something too unstable in its feverishness to feel like a paternal identification, but it may have been as close as I ever came to my father's (ruinous) passion. Gambling, in sum, was there with the unconscious. Benjamin, in his classic essay on Baudelaire, got it precisely wrong. I—shall we say?—was the good son.

*

A parenthesis on the inherent weirdness of paternal identifications . . . My oddest experience involving a paternal identification turned on my Yale dissertation, which became my first book. It was called *A Structural Study of Autobiography*, and pivoted on the chapter of Michel Leiris's multivolumed *La Règle du jeu* titled "Perséphone."[21] In *L'Age d'homme*,

Leiris had attempted an inventory of his obsessions, which sorted themselves out in terms of two symmetrical female archetypes: Lucretia, or the woman I cannot but destroy, and Judith, the woman who cannot but destroy me. *La Règle du jeu* marked a farewell to archetype, and, it seemed to me, an entry into structure. The author no longer attended to haunting images but rather to obsessive verbal fragments. He had chosen the path of free association. Thus, from Perséphone, there was a transition to *perce-oreille*, the insect known as an earwig. (Joyce was plainly on to something related when he gave his character Earwicker, in *Finnegans Wake*, the alternate name Persse O'Reilly.) But from *perce-oreille*, there was an additional transition, this time to a child's phonograph, said to be a far less "perfect" reproductive machine than his father's. And my effort in the dissertation was to demonstrate that, whereas the obsession with specular archetypes in *L'Age d'homme* had ultimately proved sterile for the autobiographer, the insistence on the verbal obsession "Perséphone" could be shown to ramify productively throughout the (then thousand) pages of Leiris's serial autobiography. In addition, "Perséphone," combining as it did the motif of the "writing machine" (or phonograph) and the phallus (his father's reproductive apparatus being more potent than his own), seemed to conjoin the two tutelary presences of my dissertation: Jacques Derrida and Jacques Lacan. The year was 1971 and the split between those two figures would soon be declared, but at the time, at least as seen from New Haven, there was a convergence whose fruitfulness had me convinced.

In the fall of 1971, Derrida read my Leiris chapter in manuscript, subsequently telling me in conversation that it was as a result of that reading that, struck by the immense deconstructive potential of Leiris's text, he had begun attending to *La Règle du jeu*. A first result of that attention was the brilliant opening of *Marges: De la philosophie*, an essay titled "Tympan," in whose margins Derrida had reproduced whole chunks of the "Perséphone" section of *La Règle du jeu*. More strikingly, Derrida had made of "Tympan" the occasion of a polemic against Lacan, now accused of "phallogocentrism." What struck me as perplexing was how Derrida could have enlisted the Leiris meditation on "Perséphone," with its plainly phallic references to a more powerful or perfect paternal machine, to underwrite an attack against phallogocentrism. The solution to my dilemma came when I consulted Derrida's text and discovered that the reference to the paternal machine had simply been elided and replaced with suspension points. I pointed out that fact in a postscript to the Leiris section of my dissertation when it was published. Derrida replied in a note that conveyed his displeasure.

In retrospect the entire episode interests me for the light it casts on the question, with which I began, of paternal identification. Perhaps it is best summarized in terms of the simultaneity of three interpretations of the phrase "the paternal reference has been cut." The first and most obvious sense refers to Derrida's suspension points: the eliminated father was Leiris's. But in declaring his hostility to Lacan in "Tympan," Derrida was taking an axe to the tutelary—or paternal—pairing that had made my dissertation possible: the eliminated father was the tandem Derrida-Lacan, that is, at some level, my own. Finally, there was admittedly my disappointment at Derrida's failure to acknowledge the role of my dissertation in revealing the deconstructive potential of "Perséphone." I had given him the dissertation in 1971; "Tympan" appeared in 1972; my dissertation was not published (by Cornell University Press) until 1974. In terms of the reference, the unacknowledged paternity was mine. Three fathers, then—Leiris père, Derrida-Lacan, and myself—managed to converge, to *mesh*, almost unthinkably, but with utter coherence, in the "Perséphone" episode. It is that quality of *unimaginable* coherence, a feature not unrelated to the absurd description of myself as Benjamin's *good* brother in the development opening onto this parenthetical excursus, which has endeared it to me and rendered it, I hope, worthy of retelling.

*

It was several years after publishing my book on Benjamin that I encountered a strange and beautiful volume by the Italian author and editor Roberto Calasso. Its title, which I find annoying and to which I'll return, is *The Ruin of Kasch*, and its subject . . . well, what *was* its subject? Calvino, who admired the book greatly, claimed it had two subjects: one was Talleyrand, and the other was everything else. It occurred to me as I read it that Calasso had in fact pulled off the feat of rewriting (and *completing*) Benjamin's legendary *Arcades Project*. For the book is an effort to generate much of the nightmare of twentieth-century Europe from a matrix supplied by the dream world of nineteenth-century Paris. Only, whereas the poles around which Benjamin organized his work were the proto-Nietzschean Baudelaire and his opposite number—"that madman who took himself for

Victor Hugo" as Cocteau called him—Victor Hugo, Calasso's comparable
figures are Talleyrand, a diplomatic sensibility too fine to be violated by a
single principle, and *his* opposite number, prize ninny and inventor, *avant
la lettre*, of the photo op, Lafayette.

It is almost as though Calasso were intent on excavating a prototype
for the axis around which the Arcades Project had been conceived. Long
before the events of February 1848, he evokes the euphoria of the Fête de
la Fédération, a year after the fall of the Bastille: "A throng of banners.
Lafayette cantering on a white horse. Three hundred priests in surplices
come forward, with acolytes in smocks and tricolor sashes. They were followed by Talleyrand, wearing his miter and leaning on his crook as he
limped along. The orchestra rang out—all twelve hundred instruments.
Passing in front of Lafayette, who had just dismounted from his steed, Talleyrand murmured to him, 'Please don't make me laugh.'"[22] And then, at
the other extreme of his book, there is the wish to go beyond Benjamin,
to offer a corrective: "Despite what Benjamin says, the great book inspired
by the arcades is not so much Aragon's *Peasant of Paris* (bewitching though
it is), but Céline's *Death on the Installment Plan*."[23] Here alone, it is suggested, do we find the "'petite musique' of gradual decomposition," "images that cannot be translated into dialectics," the "poetics of the arcades."

Now, my reason for evoking Calasso's book in this semi-autobio-
graphical context is twofold. The first is that I was stunned to find the
central conceit of virtually every one of my books prominently featured
by Calasso, who I am sure had never read me, in his remarkable tapestry:

1. My first book pretended to offer a new reading of Proust. It was
    generated from the image of biblical Abraham at a telling juncture
    in *Swann's Way*, and thus my entire reading of Proust appeared under
    an epigraph from Kafka: "I could imagine a different Abraham." The
    entire parable of Abraham is reproduced in Calasso's book on the
    French nineteenth century.

2. My second book, *Revolution and Repetition*, made much, as I have
    already suggested, of the apparent allergy to dialectic of the lumpen-
    proletariat in Marx's *Eighteenth Brumaire of Louis Bonaparte* and its
    repercussions for a reading of Victor Hugo. Calasso's book is a long
    meditation on the saving abjection of the lumpenproletariat—from
    their ancestors, the violent and rootless woodsmen and bored-silly

fishermen of eighteenth-century Massachusetts (as evoked by Talleyrand), to the "artificial barbarians" of Max Stirner, to the *gueux* of
Victor Hugo.

3. My third book, *Cataract*, bore with it a meditation on the entropic
    flow sweeping the structural (and post-structural) away in its tide,
    and here was Calasso on Talleyrand, who "soon perceived that power
    struggles would no longer take place on a chess board . . . but within a
    stream stronger than everything it swept along. This was the 'torrent'
    of which he spoke."[24] Or consider Calasso's dismissal of the structur-
    alists, the "dry priests of Judaism," who, having crossed the Red Sea,
    have vowed never to get wet again.

4. Not to mention the omnipresence of the long-forgotten Léon Bloy,
    patron saint, in his nastiness, of the lumpenproletariat, but also, in
    my reading, genuine ancestor of Lacan, and who was also beginning
    to invade much of what I wrote.

Thus, one reason for evoking Calasso is that he was beginning to supply
me with an answer to a question that intermittently haunts me: Who—
as a writer—will I have been? Answer: My books will have been a series
of very long expansions of images I would eventually find in *The Ruin
of Kasch*.

But there is a second reason for mentioning Calasso. At about the
time that *The Ruin of Kasch* was appearing in English, there appeared in
Italy a small volume by the Vatican reporter of *L'Avvenire*, one Maurizio
Blondet, who accused Calasso, who is the director of an Italian publishing house, Adelphi Edizioni, of being part of a Gnostic conspiracy with
apocalyptic designs on Western culture (through the mystico-dionysiac
venom—read: Georges Bataille—with which it had poisoned the left) and
financial designs—perhaps worth investigating for prosecution?—on the
Banca Commerciale Italiana.[25] And the specific name of the conspiracy
was Sabbatianism, or rather that subsect of Sabbatians known as Frankists,
about whom Blondet appeared to have learned from the same Scholem
essay on "Redemption Through Sin" as I had. In sum, the heuristic model
or metaphor I had chosen for my own work—*Anch'io sono sabbatiano*—
had slipped the bounds of the text—but whose text? his? mine?—and was
now being offered up as potential grounds for prosecution. Could Kafka
be far behind?

The answer is no. In 2005, Calasso published in English a rather impressive volume on Kafka called *K.* Thus, after *Kasch* and its ruin came *K.* Between the two came a well-received volume on Hindu mythology called . . . *Ka.* And before them all, at least in English, came the most famous of his works, devoted to Greek mythology, *The Marriage of Cadmus and Harmony.* So we have volumes on very disparate subjects called *Cadmo, Kasch, Ka,* and *K.* Plainly something esoteric (if not Gnostic) is in play. (In Kafka's handwriting, we are told, "the letter K plunged downward with a showy sweep the writer detested: 'I find K's ugly, almost repugnant, and yet I keep writing them; they must be very characteristic of myself.'")[26]

And it may be catching. Not long ago, I published in a literary magazine a short memoir about growing up in New York City. It appears as well in this volume. Shortly before its original publication I happened to run into the editor of the journal at a time I was running around with a copy of Calasso's Kafka book, *K.* I recommended Calasso and felt obliged to explain the strangeness of Calasso's titles.

I see, he said, and he reminded me that my memoir, named after an old sweater shop on the lower East Side of Manhattan, was called "Kandahar."

Afrancesado: Coda in Buenos Aires

Here in Buenos Aires, the "Paris of the Rio de la Plata," where thirty years of marriage to an Argentine have taken me for ever longer stays, the television announcer has just completed his advertisement for a documentary on the country's founding father with a final flourish: "Rivadavia," he proclaims, "the first of the *afrancesados*." I am struck by the honorific. In North America, after all, where *afrancesado* would probably be translated as "Frenchified," just such a term was used as a slur in a presidential election and may have played its small part in a candidate's defeat. In Paris itself, where the mock-pejorative *franchouillard* seems to trail every mention of *français*, the honorific connotations have faded. Yet here in Buenos Aires, the city's dandified mayor only recently chose to deflect the indiscreet questions of a journalist into his personal life by declaring himself *afrancesado*.

The term derives, of course, from the vicissitudes of world history. If "Frenchified" harkens back to the effeteness of the royal court, the Hispanic variant would direct us to nineteenth-century liberalism, the legacy of the French Revolution. For me, though, it is enough to see the word *afrancesado* in print for it to take on an added valence. When one's mother, however dyed-in-the-wool a New Yorker, is, as the reader may recall, named Frances, it is hard not to detect in the epithet, pointedly in the masculine, the plight of a son never completely emergent from the love of a mother long since gone. (And I am suddenly reminded of the tears with which she received a summary of my analysis of Proust, the first chapter of my disser-

tation: tears less of pride than of vulnerability, as though to cut to the quick
of Proust were inevitably, as Proust himself intuited, to be working toward
what was most exposed in one's own existence.) From a mother named
Frances, then, via thirty years of marriage, to summers (become winters) in
a city governed by a self-proclaimed *afrancesado*. One has to imagine Oedipus as a happy man.

*

*(There are other, labyrinthine paths that have no doubt brought me here
to the Paris of the South. I have long been intrigued by the fact that Virginia
Woolf's* Orlando *was translated into Spanish by Borges, Alicia's blind teacher,
and into French by Charles Mauron, my blind teacher, whom I discussed in
"Chiasmus." In which novel,* Orlando *encounters love when a figure of "extraordinary seductiveness" approaches him one "seventh of January," the day
that would later be our wedding anniversary. The dream: to one day write a
memoir of my marriage in the form of a comparative study of the Spanish and
French translations of* Orlando . . .)*

*

Buenos Aires, it will be sensed, is a city of psychoanalysis, perhaps the
last remaining city on the planet in which "Freudian" (like "French") is an
unalloyed honorific. I well recall a first taxi ride, twenty years ago, through
the city's downtown. Passing before an impressive building on the Calle
Corrientes, I asked the driver to identify it. The answer was memorable:
"That, sir, is the Teatro San Martín. You can find anything there: theater,
movies, lectures on Lacan." (Lacan, it will be recalled, whom I had translated at the beginning of my career in an issue of the series Yale French Studies titled *French Freud*: the sauce, or the plot, thickens . . .) Upon returning
to Boston, I recounted the cabby's words to Christopher R***, the eminent British critic who has already surfaced in these pages. His response was
equally unforgettable: "It sounds like my idea of hell." It was enough for me
to report his rejoinder to an Argentine analyst on a subsequent trip for the
quip to bear fruit. A year later the analyst's brief history of psychoanalysis in
Argentina, titled "A Certain Idea of Hell," would arrive in the mail.

The city's devotion to Freud and his legacy is striking. But perhaps
it is the multilingual medium of that devotion that is more remarkable

still. During an early trip to Argentina, it was sufficient for a local daily to learn that a sometime translator of Lacan was in town for it to run a two-page interview with me, evoking the aforementioned issue of Yale French Studies, under the title "Historia del French Freud." True, Buenos Aires is famously a city of Spanish-speaking Italians, dressing like the British and thinking of themselves as French, but the combination of French, English, Spanish, and Viennese in that headline touched me, as though the city had managed to custom-tailor (another *porteño* specialty!) its multicultural essence to my specific circumstance.

The interlingual as the privileged medium of the unconscious . . . Not far down the street from our apartment in Buenos Aires is a colorfully named psychoanalytic institute, the Círculo Descartes. For anyone attuned to Cartesian notions of the sovereign thinking subject, the name seems a misnomer. Stare at the nameplate a bit longer, though, allowing the French name to absorb the Spanish encroaching on it from every quarter, and its name metamorphoses into a common noun: *descartes*, meaning "discards." Yes, one agrees, the sovereign subject, a mirage grounded in the psychic refuse—dreams, jokes, slips of the tongue—of mental life. Has there ever been a more economical, more capacious encapsulation of the psychoanalytic perspective than that interlingual pun? Working the French-German border, I once, in an essay on Proust, for heuristic purposes, told a joke about the self-denigrating Jew Katzmann, who decides to Gallicize his name and becomes, self-defeatingly, Monsieur Chat-l'homme (Shalom). Amusingly interlingual, but ultimately too narrowly Oedipal to encompass the analytic essence grasped by the French-Spanish pun encountered on a nameplate in Buenos Aires.

It has been said that the reason that the Jews of eastern Europe became great experts in French culture was that in their urge, after emancipation, to partake of Enlightenment, which for them meant *Aufklärung* or Germany, they felt an obligation to try harder, to be even more Western than the Germans—which meant waxing French. Perhaps, then, this displacement from French-German to French-Spanish is the next step: a further westering of the assimilationist project, now arrived in a Buenos Aires become the last stronghold of Francophilia.

The essay on Proust which I began with the Katzmann/Shalom joke was titled "Literature and Collaboration" and dealt with Proust's curious relations with Jacques Benoist-Méchin, who would end up the disgraced

architect of Vichy's proposed collaboration with the Nazis and later attempt to explain the error of his ways in a volume on Proust.[1] (Might my
mother's tears, upon hearing my first analysis of Proust, have been more
prescient than I imagined?) That circumstance is a reminder of a further
valence of *afrancesado* that has significant resonances with my work. *Afrancesado*, after all, was the term of abuse applied to those adepts of French
liberalism in Spain who eventually became collaborators with the Napoleonic occupation. France's own collaborators (with the Nazis) would seize
on the irony—or attenuating circumstance—of a Francophile collaboration. Indeed the most talented of them, Paul Morand, wrote his longest
novel, *Le Flagellant de Séville*, which I have analyzed in a long essay titled
"Flowers of Evil," in expansion of the parallel.[2]

   With the *afrancesado*, the idealist "Frances-ed" over, become collaborator, I approach a motif that has already surfaced in this volume, the Sabbatian will to enter into evil in order to defeat it from within. No need to
indicate more at this point than the centrality of that trope (or fantasy) in
much of my later writing. It is not for nothing, I take it, that a line out of
Paul Morand introduces what is the central essay in this volume, "Chiasmus." The motif also brings me back, but more deeply because more am-
biguously, to the fantasy of resistance with which this book begins. To end
where one began . . . It is a brisk August day in Buenos Aires. I can think
of nothing I'd rather do than head to my favorite café, a luminous, uncluttered establishment of the sort one can barely find anymore in Paris, to
pursue that ambiguity. Café Martínez is located, as it happens, around the
corner from our apartment in Barrio Norte, on the Calle French.

Acknowledgments

I've been lucky enough to find myself writing more and more from a place in which *Denken* and *Danken*, to recall Heidegger's pun, thinking and thanking, coincide. Indeed, much of this volume has been written, visibly, from within just such an overlap. Yet because these chapters tend to focus on moments of surprise or quirkiness, I have no doubt made insufficient mention of a number of friends who have sustained my work over the years: Arthur Goldhammer, whose brilliance has long been a special source of enlightenment on matters French; Régis Debray, the incandescence of whose prose has helped me to keep the faith; Christopher Maurer, whose wry stewardship of the Boston University Romance Studies Department has had me whistling Mozart's *Maurerfreude* more than once on the way to work; Denis Hollier, the genius of whose wit has had me smiling since the time we served as colleagues at Berkeley in 1974; Pierre-Emmanuel Dauzat, whose theoretical and practical guidance through the intricacies of French intellectual life have been an ongoing boon; Bruno Chaouat, whose incisive interest in my work has helped keep me going.

My children, Natalia and Ezra, surface here and there in these pages, but I would be remiss if I failed to acknowledge explicitly the generous ear with which they have taken in—and refused to be taken in by—a number of the "adventures" gathered above. As for Alicia Borinsky, to whom the book is dedicated, the alertness and imagination with which she has accompanied me through these episodes so far surpasses my own capacity to bring to her own achievements resources of mind worthy of them that I am inclined to close these remarks by reciting to her one more time, in the words of Lorenzo da Ponte, "Contessa, perdono."

Notes

PREFACE

1. To bring that sensibility to bear on one's sense of self is the opposite of issuing an *apologia pro vita sua*. For which reason I have resisted including my version of a tenure struggle, mentioned in passing in these pages, that both scandalized and titillated the "profession" in the late seventies. I did, however, write it up. Perhaps some day I will publish my polemical piece "Of Tartuffe in Baltimore." For the moment I would summarize its argument with Lord Holland's quip, in the eighteenth century, in response to the description of an act of skullduggery as a "pious fraud": "I can see the fraud, but where is the piety?"

CHAPTER 2

1. George Steiner, *Errata: An Examined Life* (London: Weidenfeld & Nicolson, 1997), p. 61.
2. Will Rogers, "Glamor Pusses," *Time*, September 9, 1946, p. 24.
3. Jo Davidson, *Between Sittings: An Informal Autobiography* (New York: Dial Press, 1951), p. 118. Page references in the text are to this edition.
4. Cited in Graham Robb, *Balzac: A Life* (New York: Norton, 1994), p. 205.
5. *Time*, September 9, 1946, p. 23.
6. *The Life and Times of Sadakichi Hartmann, 1867–1944* (Riverside, CA: Riverside Press-Enterprise Co., 1970), frontispiece. Published in conjunction with the exhibit shown at the University of California, Riverside.

CHAPTER 3

Portions of this chapter were previously published as "Truth in New York" in *French Politics and Society* 15:2 (Spring 1997).
1. Jacques Habert, *Verrazane: Quand New York s'appelait Angoulême* (Paris: Perrin, 1993), p. 120.

CHAPTER 4

An earlier version of this chapter appeared as "The Boston/Vichy Connection" in *Salmagundi* 135–136 (Summer–Fall 2002).

1. Eric Conan and Henri Rousso, *Vichy, un passé qui ne passe pas* (Paris: Fayard, 1994), p. 75.

2. Alain Finkielkraut, *Une voix qui vient de l'autre rive* (Paris: Gallimard, 2000), p. 67.

3. Pierre-André Taguieff, *Résister au bougisme: Démocratie forte contre mondialisation techno-marchande* (Paris: Mille et Une Nuits, 2001), p. 103.

4. Marc Fumaroli, *L'Etat culturel: Essai sur une religion moderne* (Paris: Fallois, 1991), p. 112.

5. *New Grove Dictionary of Music and Musicians*, vol. 17, eds. Stanley Sadie and John Tyrrell, (Oxford: Oxford University Press, 2003), p. 387.

6. Charles Munch, *Je suis un chef d'orchestre* (Paris: Editions du Conquistador, 1954), p. 26.

7. *Baker's Biographical Dictionary of Musicians*, ed. Nicolas Slonimsky (New York: Schirmer, 2000), p. 2547.

8. Munch, *Je suis un chef,* p. 31.

9. Miriam Chimènes, ed., *La Vie musicale sous Vichy* (Paris: Editions Complexe, 2001).

10. Chimènes, *La Vie musicale,* pp. 143, 225, 217. Alexandra Laedrich (p. 225) lists Reynaldo Hahn as one of the banned composers, and yet his operetta *Ciboulette* was slated for performance on July 9, 1942, at the Grand Casino of Vichy (p. 405). The operetta was positively reviewed by Honegger when it was performed at Marigny in December 1941. See "Reprise de *Ciboulette,*" *Comoedia,* no. 28, December 27, 1941–January 3, 1942.

11. Ibid., p. 144.

12. Leslie Sprout, "Les Commandes de Vichy, aube d'une ère nouvelle," in Chimènes, *La Vie musicale,* p. 173. The commission to compose the cantata actually came through in the springtime of 1940, just prior to the fall of France, but since support, composition, and performance all occurred during the Vichy years, Sprout's decision to discuss the work as a "Vichy commission" appears justified.

13. On Mallarmé's debt to Max Müller, see Bertrand Marchal, *La Religion de Mallarmé* (Paris: Corti, 1988).

14. See Claudine Gothot-Mirsch's edition of Leconte de Lisle's *Poèmes antiques* (Paris: Gallimard, 1994), p. 321.

15. Paul Landormy, *La Musique française après Debussy* (Paris: Gallimard, 1943), p. 217.

16. Sprout, "Les Commandes de Vichy," p. 176.

17. Chimènes, *La Vie musicale,* p. 20. This appears to overlook, among others, the case of the writer Paul Morand, Vichy's ambassador to Bucharest, then Berne.

18. Ibid., p. 46.

19. Paul Morand, *Journal inutile*, vol. 2 (Paris: Gallimard, 2001), p. 344.

20. Chimènes, *La Vie musicale*, p. 41.

21. Geneviève Honegger, *Charles Munch: Un chef d'orchestre dans le siècle* (Strasbourg: La Nuée Bleue, 1992), p. 156.

22. Jean-Philippe Mousnier, *Paul Paray* (Paris: L'Harmattan, 1998), p. 164.

23. Honegger, *Charles Munch*, p. 164.

24. Chimènes, *La Vie musicale*, p. 30.

25. By war's end, Munch may even have been able to flaunt a brief pro forma association with the Resistance. See Guy Krivopissko and Daniel Virieux, "Musiciens: Une profession en résistance?" in Chimènes, *La Vie musicale*, p. 339. Neither Manuel Rosenthal nor Henri Dutilleux could recall Munch's presence at the Comité du Front national des musiciens, a group with Resistance sympathies.

26. François Dufay, *Le Voyage d'automne: Octobre 1941, des écrivains français en Allemagne* (Paris: Plon, 2000), p. 224.

27. Munch, *Je suis un chef*, p. 11.

28. Frances Stonor Saunders, *The Cultural Cold War* (New York: New Press, 1999), p. 117.

29. See my "Structuralism, Poetry, Music: Lévi-Strauss Between Mallarmé and Wagner" in *The Cambridge Companion to Lévi-Strauss*, ed. Boris Wiseman (Cambridge: Cambridge University Press, 2009), pp. 257–264.

CHAPTER 5

An earlier version of this chapter was published in *Agni* 52 (2000).

CHAPTER 6

An earlier version of this chapter was published in *Agni* 61 (2005).

CHAPTER 7

An earlier version of this chapter was published as "Chiasmus: A Memoir" in *Parallax* 22 (January 2002); reprinted with permission.

1. Paul Morand, *Venises* (Paris: Gallimard, 1971), p. 9.

2. My translation of Lacan's "Seminar on 'The Purloined Letter'" first appeared in *French Freud*, Yale French Studies 48 (1973); subsequently in *Aesthetics Today*, ed. Morris Philipson and Paul Gudel (New York: New American Library, 1980), pp. 382–412, and *The Purloined Poe*, ed. John Muller and William Richardson (Baltimore: Johns Hopkins University Press, 1987), pp. 28–54.

3. Walter Benjamin, "Stamp Scams," trans. Jeffrey Mehlman, *London Review of Books*, September 8, 1994, p. 16.

4. Jeffrey Mehlman, "Orphée scripteur: Blanchot, Rilke, Derrida," *Poétique* 20 (1974), pp. 458–482.

5. Jeffrey Mehlman, *Legacies: Of Anti-Semitism in France* (Minneapolis: University of Minnesota Press, 1983).

6. For a contemporary, partisan account of the "revolutionary" success of *La France juive*, see Léon Daudet, *Paris vécu*, vol. 9 (Paris: Gallimard, 1969), p. 243.

7. Jeffrey Mehlman, "Of Literature and Terror: Blanchot at *Combat*," in "Les Années 30, *MLN* 95 (1980), pp. 808–829.

8. Bernard-Henri Lévy, "La gauche, telle quelle," *Le Matin*, June 22, 1982.

9. Mathieu Bénézet, "Maurice Blanchot, Céline, and *Tel Quel*," *La Quinzaine littéraire*, July 1–15, 1982.

10. In his exhaustive biography, *Maurice Blanchot, partenaire invisible* (Seyssel: Champ Vallon, 1998), Christophe Bident reveals that Blanchot was royally paid by the Vichy regime as a literary functionary in the cultural bureaucracy Jeune France, but was generally perceived as not doing much of a job. Perhaps that lack of zeal should be chalked up to "resistance." See my review of Bident, "Vie et oeuvre de Maurice Blanchot: Le Partage du mythe," *Critique* 630 (November 1999), pp. 942–952.

11. Jeffrey Mehlman, "Lettre à Maurice Nadeau," *L'Infini*, no. 1 (January 1983).

12. Jean Laplanche, *Life and Death in Psychoanalysis*, translated and with an introduction by Jeffrey Mehlman (Baltimore: Johns Hopkins University Press, 1976).

13. The notion that anti-Semitism might not "disfigure" a poet's work but positively "animate" or enliven it has been argued, in the case of T. S. Eliot (a significant influence during my undergraduate years) by Anthony Julius, *T. S. Eliot: Anti-Semitism and Literary Form* (Cambridge: Cambridge University Press, 1995), p. 173. Concerning the "treble" and "bass" components of Eliot's work, Louis Menand has supplied equivalents in his twin genealogies of the poet: on the one hand, Eliot becomes a *symboliste* in 1908 after discovering Laforgue while reading Arthur Symons's *The Symbolist Movement in Literature* in the Harvard Union; on the other, Eliot discovers the allures of French anti-Semitism in the writings of Charles Maurras, recommended to him by his Harvard professor Irving Babbitt. See Louis Menand, *American Studies* (New York: Farrar, Straus & Giroux, 2002), pp. 58–64.

14. "Ce que disaient les trois cigognes," in Henri Mondor, *Mallarmé plus intime* (Paris: Gallimard, 1944); republished in *Documents Stéphane Mallarmé*, vol. 3, ed. Carl Paul Barbier (Paris: Nizet, 1971).

15. Charles Mauron, *Introduction à la psychanalyse de Mallarmé* (Neuchâtel: La Baconnière, 1950).

16. Charles Mauron, *L'Inconscient dans l'oeuvre et la vie de Racine* (Gap: Ophrys, 1957).

17. For an extrapolation of these thoughts on Racine to a reading of Wallace Stevens's "The Figure of the Youth as Virile Poet," see my "Thoughts on Wal-

lace Stevens' Contribution at Pontigny-en-Amérique: Response to Cavell," and Stanley Cavell, "Postscript: Response to Mehlman," in *Artists, Intellectuals, and World War II: The Pontigny Encounters at Mount Holyoke College, 1942–1944*, ed. Christopher Benfey and Karen Remmler (Amherst: University of Massachusetts Press, 2006), pp. 80–88.

18. Paul Valéry, "Lettre sur Mallarmé," *Variété*, vol. 2 (Paris: Gallimard, 1930), p. 285.

19. Cited in Mary Ann Caws and Sarah Bird Wright, *Bloomsbury and France: Art and Friends* (New York: Oxford University Press, 2000), p. 274.

20. Ibid., p. 273.

21. Virginia Woolf, *Roger Fry: A Biography* (New York: Harcourt Brace Jovanovich, 1940), p. 276.

22. Ibid., p. 284.

23. Quentin Bell, *Bloomsbury Recalled* (New York: Columbia University Press, 1995), pp. 114–115.

24. *The Letters of Virginia Woolf*, vol. 6, ed. Nigel Nicolson and Joanne Trautmann (New York: Harcourt Brace Jovanovich, 1980), p. 84.

25. Caws and Wright, *Bloomsbury and France*, p. 281.

26. *Letters of Virginia Woolf*, vol. 6, p. 487.

27. Mauron's first wife was the writer and Provençal folklorist Marie Mauron. Mauron himself was coauthor with Camille Dourguin, of *Lou Prouvençau a l'Escolo* (Saint-Rémy-de-Provence: Lou Prouvençau a l'Escolo, 1952), a school text intended to keep the waning language of the South alive.

28. Caws and Wright, *Bloomsbury and France*, p. 280.

29. E. M. Forster, *Two Cheers for Democracy* (New York: Harcourt Brace, 1966), p. 132.

30. Ibid., p. 342.

31. *Selected Letters of E. M. Forster*, vol. 2, ed. Mary Lago and P. N. Furbank (Cambridge, MA: Harvard University Press, 1985), p. 182.

32. E. M. Forster, *Commonplace Book*, ed. Philip Gardner (Stanford: Stanford University Press, 1985), p. 324.

33. Note, however, that after the war, in the course of a review of Mauron's *L'Homme triple*, Forster was plainly happy to be able to report on Mauron's activities during the war: "With the war and the German occupation he took part in the resistance movement. The German Africa Corps at one time actually encamped in the olive fields round his house. When the Germans went, his life changed dramatically: he was summoned by his fellow citizens to be Mayor of St Rémy as his father had been before him, and he showed in those difficult days the tolerance, courage and humanity which one finds in his writings, together with great administrative ability." "Charles Mauron and 'L'Homme Triple,'" *Adam International Review* 200 (1949), pp. 18–19. Forster's essay says of

Mauron's book: "Those are the words I was waiting for, and would have spoken myself had I known how."

34. Lionel Trilling, *E. M. Forster* (New York: New Directions, 1943), p. 168.

35. E. M. Forster, *Aspects of the Novel* (New York: Harcourt Brace, 1927), p. 153.

36. Ibid., p. 156.

37. Ibid., p. 158.

38. Ibid., p. 159.

39. Ibid., p. 164.

40. Philip Fisher, "One of the Master Texts of a Whole Generation," in *Redrawing the Boundaries: The Transformation of English and American Literary Studies*, ed. Stephen Greenblatt and Giles Gunn (New York: Modern Language Association, 1992), p. 235.

41. Frederick Crews, *E. M. Forster: The Perils of Humanism* (Princeton, NJ: Princeton University Press, 1962), p. 80: "Lionel Trilling is right in comparing *Where Angels Fear to Tread* to *The Ambassadors*, both novels being concerned with 'the effect of a foreign country and a strange culture upon insular ideas and provincial personalities.'"

42. E. M. Forster, "Notes on English Character," in *Abinger Harvest* (New York: Harcourt Brace Jovanovich, 1936), p. 7.

43. E. M. Forster, *Where Angels Fear to Tread* (New York: Vintage, 1992), p. 179.

44. Since Pasiphae, who passes herself off as a cow in order to satisfy her tragic lust, has surfaced as presiding deity of the *Aspects/Racine* nexus, it may be appropriate, at this juncture, to mention Mauron's riveting philosophical discussion, "The Cow," published in 1933 in T. S. Eliot's *Criterion*. Inspired by the philosophical discussion of idealism at the beginning of Forster's *The Longest Journey*, it would subordinate the subject/object distinction to the perceptual event "The-Sight-of-a-Cow." "Why do away with 'see'?" writes Mauron, who at the time was sinking into blindness.

45. Henry James, *Letters*, vol. 4, ed. Leon Edel (Cambridge, MA: Harvard University Press, 1984), pp. 302–303.

46. Henry James, *The Ambassadors* (New York: Norton, 1994), p. 65.

47. Jeffrey Mehlman, *A Structural Study of Autobiography: Proust, Leiris, Sartre, Lévi-Strauss* (Ithaca, NY: Cornell University Press, 1974).

48. Jeffrey Mehlman, *Emigré New York: French Intellectuals in Wartime Manhattan, 1940–1944* (Baltimore: Johns Hopkins University Press, 2000).

49. Postscript (2009): One measure of a reading's value is its ability to generate still other readings. In the case of "Chiasmus," the point was driven home to me, in the time since its completion, at both extremes of the text:

    1. Boston 1983 and the "Blanchot affair": In 2006, Angie David published a full-length biography of Dominique Aury, the pseudonymous author—as "Pauline Réage"—of the 1954 classic of erotic literature, *Histoire*

d'O. Dominique Aury was for twenty-five years a leading figure (and the only woman) in the inner sanctum of the Gallimard publishing house. Upon consulting the book's table of contents (at the suggestion of a colleague), I was stunned to find a chapter entitled "Jeffrey Mehlman, 'Blanchot à Combat.'" The explanation? In charting Blanchot's transition from the prewar anti-Semitic journal *Combat* to a milieu with important links to the Resistance, I had identified two tutelary figures: Thierry Maulnier, who edited the fascist-prone *Combat* in 1936, and Jean Paulhan, who was a leading figure in the intellectual Resistance. As it happens, the (clandestine) author of the erotic classic had successive clandestine love affairs with Thierry Maulnier (during his years with *Combat*) and Jean Paulhan (as of the period of his involvement with the Resistance). And these affairs were the sequences around which David's biography was organized. Moreover, Aury's principal epistolary confidant during both affairs appears to have been none other than Maurice Blanchot, who had fallen under her spell. In brief, my ethico-political essay on Blanchot, the subject of a polemic in 1983, had turned out to offer, unwittingly, a scenario of sorts for David's biography of Aury. Unless, of course, it meant that my ethico-political reading of a major transition in Blanchot's life might be better read as the record (or reflection) of a sentimental—or even lovelorn—friendship.

2. At the other extreme (and no less under the sign of sex and its taboos), Cambridge 1927 and E. M. Forster. Consider his classic novel of 1910, *Howards End*, and the hidden complexity informing it when read with an eye to chiasmus (or the pattern of the hourglass, as Forster calls it). The novel comes with its own built-in ideology ("Only connect . . ."). The connection is famously that between the aesthete Schlegels and the philistine Wilcoxes, the "monk" and the "beast" in us all, as the author puts it. Yet from the novel's perspective the marriage of a Schlegel (sister) to a Wilcox (patriarch) accomplishes nothing and is but a way station toward another "connection," one that sees the two Schlegel sisters moving into the country house of the title, there to raise the illegitimate son one of them has borne through a coupling with the lamentable (and mercifully deceased) Leonard Bast. Turn now to *Where Angels Fear to Tread*, the James-inspired novel evoked in passing near the end of "Chiasmus." At a key juncture, Philip Herriton, after the accidental death of the child his deceased sister-in-law, Lilia, had borne to her Italian lover Gino, undergoes an experience of intensely physical, even sadistic, communion with the enraged Gino, an experience which appears to bring him as close to authenticity as the sad young Englishman will come in his life. And then he returns, defeated, to his mother in England. In sum, *Howards End* and *Where Angels Fear to Tread* together form a chiasmus. 1905: an unconsummated same-sex union around the life of a child cut short and beginning as a Brit's flight from matriarchy to

the genuineness of Italy. 1910: a same-sex couple—the sisters Schlegel—formed in the transgressive epiphany of a kiss, a living rebuke to the Wilcox patriarchy, will thrive at Howards End while raising the deceased Leonard's child. Homo-parentality, in sum, a word that did not even exist when Forster wrote his novels, as the core fantasy around which they were writtten . . .

CHAPTER 8

Portions of this chapter were originally published as "Derrida: Notes Toward a Memoir" in *SubStance* 34, no. 1 (2005). © 2005 by the Board of Regents of the University of Wisconsin System. Reproduced courtesy of the University of Wisconsin Press.

1. John Searle, "Reiterating the Differences," *Glyph* 1 (1977), pp. 198–208.
2. Jacques Derrida, "Limited Inc," *Glyph* 2 (1977), pp. 162–254.
3. Jeffrey Mehlman, "Writing and Deference: The Politics of Literary Adulation," *Representations* 15 (Summer 1986), pp. 1–14.
4. Jeffrey Mehlman, "Deconstructing de Man's Life," *Newsweek*, February 15, 1988, p. 64.

CHAPTER 9

1. Mel Gussow and Charles McGrath, "Saul Bellow, Who Breathed Life into American Novel, Dies at 89," *New York Times*, April 6, 2005.
2. James Atlas, *Bellow: A Biography* (New York: Random House, 2000), p. 411.
3. Gussow and McGrath, "Saul Bellow Dies at 89."
4. Atlas, *Bellow*, p. 322.
5. Ibid., p. 554.
6. Saul Bellow, *From Jerusalem and Back* (New York: Viking, 1976), p. 127.
7. Cited in Atlas, *Bellow*, p. 191.

CHAPTER 10

1. Jeffrey Mehlman, "Steiner l'antinomique," *Cahiers de l'Herne*, ed. Pierre-Emmanuel Dauzat (Paris: Editions de l'Herne, 2003), pp. 77–88.
2. George Steiner, *No Passion Spent: Essays 1978–1995* (New Haven, CT: Yale University Press, 1996), pp. 68–69.
3. Ibid., p. 231.
4. See Michel-Antoine Burnier and Cécile Romane, *Le Secret de l'abbé Pierre* (Paris: Editions Mille et Une Nuits, 1996), p. 7, where particular attention is paid to the following passage from l'abbé Pierre's letter of April 15, 1996, to Roger Garaudy: "But with the Book of Joshua, I discovered how a genuine 'Shoah' affecting all life in the Promised Land was carried out."

5. See Brigitte Hamann, *Hitler's Vienna: A Dictator's Apprenticeship* (New York: Oxford University Press, 1999), p. 62.

6. *Errata: An Examined Life* (London: Weidenfeld & Nicholson, 1997), p. 70.

7. Jeffrey Mehlman, "George Steiner at the Lycée Français," in *Emigré New York: French Intellectuals in Wartime Manhattan, 1940–1944* (Baltimore: Johns Hopkins University Press, 2000), pp. 104–116.

8. George Steiner, *The Deeps of the Sea and Other Fiction* (London: Faber & Faber, 1996), p. 142.

9. Mehlman, "George Steiner at the Lycée," p. 111.

10. Steiner, *Errata*, pp. 28, 36.

11. See Jeffrey Mehlman, *Legacies: Of Anti-Semitism in France* (Minneapolis: University of Minnesota Press, 1983), p. 53, and Michael Marrus and Robert Paxton, *Vichy et les Juifs* (Paris: Calmann-Lévy, 1981).

12. George Steiner and Ramin Jahanbegloo, *Entretiens* (Paris: Editions du Félin, 1992), p. 144.

13. George Steiner, *Language and Silence* (New York: Atheneum, 1977), p. 130.

14. Ibid., p. 128.

15. Ibid., p. 139.

16. Ibid., p. 139.

17. Jeffrey Mehlman, "Core of the Core: A Phantasmagoria in Translation," *Comparative Literature* 49, no. 1 (Winter 1997), pp. 1–23.

18. Steiner, *Language and Silence*, p. 133.

19. Steiner and Jahanbegloo, *Entretiens*, p. 22.

20. Steiner, *Language and Silence*, p. 140.

21. Ibid., p. 145.

22. Steiner, *The Deeps of the Sea*, p. 393.

23. Ibid., p. 391.

24. Steiner, *Language and Silence*, p. 147.

25. Even as Rebatet, rabid fascist and best-selling writer of the Occupation, was the author, following the war, of what Steiner regards as one of the "secret masterpieces" of the twentieth century, *Les Deux étendards*. See George Steiner, *Extraterritorial* (New York: Atheneum, 1971), p. 45, and *Errata*, p. 138.

26. Pierre Boutang and George Steiner, *Dialogues: Sur le mythe d'Antigone, sur le sacrifice d'Abraham* (Paris: J. C. Lattès, 1994), pp. 29, 139.

27. Ibid., p. 43.

28. Steiner, *Errata*, p. 138.

29. Boutang and Steiner, *Dialogues*, p. 10.

30. Boutang, in point of fact, left France for Morocco in 1942 and ended up championing the accession of the comte de Paris to the throne as an alternative to both Pétain and de Gaulle. See Stéphane Giocanti's preface to Boutang, *Les Abeilles de Delphes* (Paris: Editions des Syrtes, 1999), p. 11.

31. Boutang and Steiner, *Dialogues*, pp. 136–137.

32. Boutang, *Les Abeilles de Delphes*, p. 324.

33. Ibid., p. 325.

34. Ibid., p. 326.

35. Gabriel Marcel, *Cinq pièces majeures* (Paris: Plon, 1973), p. 469.

36. Steiner and Jahanbegloo, *Entretiens*, p. 23.

37. See ibid., p. 30.

38. Boutang and Steiner, *Dialogues*, p. 43.

39. Steiner, *Errata*, p. 139.

40. George Steiner, "'Logocrats' (A Note on de Maistre, Heidegger, and Pierre Boutang)," in *Langage et politique* (Brussels: European University Institute, 1982), p. 74.

41. Ibid., p. 68.

42. George Steiner, *Martin Heidegger* (New York: Viking, 1978), p. 158.

43. Boutang, *Les Abeilles de Delphes*, p. 112.

44. George Santayana, *Reason in Religion* (New York: Collier, 1962), p. 58.

45. Santayana, *Persons and Places* (Cambridge, MA: MIT Press, 1987), p. 502.

46. Boutang, *La République de Joinovici* (Paris: Amiot-Dumont, 1949), p. 38. On Joinovici, see also André Goldschmidt, *L'Affaire Joinovici: Collaborateur, résistant et . . . bouc émissaire* (Toulouse: Privat, 2002), a book which curiously makes no reference to Boutang's work.

47. Boutang, *La République de Joinovici*, p. 12.

48. Ibid., p. 115.

49. See Mehlman, *Legacies*, pp. 16–22, and the first section of Chapter 7 of this book.

50. Boutang, *La République de Joinovici*, p. 15.

51. Boutang, *Les Abeilles de Delphes*, p. 14.

52. Steiner, *Errata*, p. 141.

53. Boutang, *Les Abeilles de Delphes*, p. 234

54. See François Huguenin, *A l'école de l'Action française: Un siècle de vie intellectuelle* (Paris: J. C. Lattès, 1998), p. 536.

55. Boutang and Steiner, *Dialogues*, p. 153.

56. See Steiner, "The Remembrancer," *TLS*, October 8, 1993.

57. Boutang, *La République de Joinovici*, pp. 40, 61.

58. Ibid., p. 48.

59. Irving Wohlfarth, "De l'historien comme chiffonnier," in Heinz Weismann, *Walter Benjamin et Paris* (Paris: Cerf, 1986), p. 566. "Might not the messiah, who is so often depicted as a beggar, just as well appear as a ragpicker?"

60. Boutang, *Les Abeilles de Delphes*, p. 325.

61. See Mehlman, *Legacies*, pp. 42–43.

62. See Jeffrey Mehlman, "Flowers of Evil: Paul Morand, the Collaboration, and Literary History," in *Genealogies of the Text: Literature, Psychoanalysis, and Politics in Modern France* (Cambridge: Cambridge University Press, 1995), pp. 212–216.

CHAPTER 12

1. Jean Genet, *Un captif amoureux* (Paris: Gallimard, 1986), p. 150. Page references in the text are to this edition.

2. Edmund White, *Genet: A Biography* (New York: Knopf, 1993), p. 627.

3. François Regnault, "Le Choix d'Homère," in *Genet à Chatila*, ed. Jérôme Hankins (Paris: Babel, 1992), p. 194.

4. On that intervention, in London, see my *Genealogies of the Text: Literature, Psychoanalysis, and Politics in Modern France* (Cambridge: Cambridge University Press, 1995), p. 217.

5. Romain Gary, *Chien blanc* (Paris: Gallimard, 1970), p. 141. See my "*Chien blanc*: Panthères noires et lettres françaises," in *The Florence Gould Lectures at New York University*, vol. 8, edited by Tom Bishop with Coralie Girard (New York: New York Center for French Civilization and Culture at New York University, 2007).

6. Eric Marty, *Bref séjour à Jerusalem* (Paris: Gallimard, 2003).

7. Ibid., p. 182.

8. Claude Lanzmann, "Vingt ans après," *Les Temps modernes* 622 (December 2002–January 2003).

9. Jeffrey Mehlman, *Legs de l'anti-sémitisme en France* (Paris: Denoël, 1984).

10. Marty, *Bref séjour*, p. 19.

11. Jean Genet, *L'Ennemi déclaré: Textes et entretiens*, ed. Albert Dichy (Paris: Gallimard, 1991), p. 254.

12. Ibid., pp. 261–262.

13. Ibid., p. 257.

14. Ibid., p. 264.

15. Marty, *Bref séjour*, p. 139.

16. Genet, *L'Ennemi déclaré*, p. 149.

17. Jean Genet, *Pompes funèbres* (Paris: Gallimard, 1953), p. 262.

18. Hankins, *Genet à Chatila*, p. 81.

19. Didier Eribon, *Une morale du minoritaire: Variations sur un thème de Jean Genet* (Paris: Fayard, 2001).

20. Alain Milianti, "Le Fils de la honte," in Hankins, *Genet à Chatila*, pp. 174–175.

21. Eribon, *Une morale du minoritaire*, pp. 41, 27.

22. Genet, *Pompes funèbres*, p. 78.

CHAPTER 13

Reprinted from the Harvard and Radcliffe Class of 1965 Twenty-fifth and Forti-eth Anniversary Reports by permission of the Harvard Alumni Association Class Report Office.

CHAPTER 14

1. Régis Debray, *Contretemps* (Paris: Gallimard, 1992), p. 18.

CHAPTER 15

1. Louis Wolfson, *Le Schizo et les langues ou la phonétique chez le psychotique* (Paris: Gallimard, 1970).

2. Jeffrey Mehlman, "Portnoy in Paris," *Diacritics* 2, no. 4 (1972), pp. 21–28.

3. Philip Roth, *Portnoy's Complaint* (New York: Random House, 1969), pp. 167–168.

4. *Postscript*: Louis Wolfson did not show up on that occasion, during which Pontalis and I engaged in a spirited exchange on Wolfson and such other matters as the analyst's recasting of the fraternal relation in terms of *frérocité*. See my "Sur Pontalis écrivain" and J.-B. Pontalis, "Réponse à Jeffrey Mehlman" in J.-B. Pontalis et al., *Passé présent: Dialoguer avec J.-B. Pontalis*, ed. Jacques André (Paris: P.U.F., 2007). Subsequently, Pontalis has prefaced *Dossier Wolfson ou l'affaire du Schizo et les langues* (Paris: Gallimard, 2009), which includes a number of provocative texts arguing the significance of Wolfson's achievement, by J. M. G. Le Clézio, Paul Auster, Michel Foucault, and others.

CHAPTER 16

1. Walter Benjamin, *Briefe*, vol. 2, ed. Gershom Scholem and Theodor W. Adorno (Frankfurt: Suhrkamp, 1978), p. 862.

2. Terry Eagleton, *Walter Benjamin, or Towards a Revolutionary Criticism* (London: Verso, 1981), p. 162.

3. John-Paul Sartre, *Mallarmé: La Lucidité et sa face d'ombre* (Paris: Gallimard, 1986), p. 28.

4. See my "Weininger in a Poem by Apollinaire," in *Jews and Gender: Responses to Otto Weininger*, ed. Nancy Harrowitz and Barbara Hyams (Philadelphia: Temple University Press, 1994).

5. Gershom Scholem, "Redemption Through Sin," in *The Messianic Idea in Judaism* (New York: Schocken, 1971).

6. Gershom Scholem, "Walter Benjamin and His Angel," in *On Jews and Judaism in Crisis: Selected Essays*, ed. Werner J. Dannhauser (Schocken: New York, 1976), pp. 198–236.

7. Jeffrey Mehlman, *Walter Benjamin for Children: An Essay on His Radio Years* (Chicago: University of Chicago Press, 1993).

8. Scholem, *On Jews and Judaism*, p. 213.

9. Walter Benjamin, *Gesammelte Schriften*, vol. 1 (Frankfurt: Suhrkamp, 1980), p. 518. Subsequent notes in the text are to the Suhrkamp edition.

10. In Benjamin, *Gesammelte Schriften,* ibid., p. 696.

11. "Baudelaire with Freud: Theory and Pain," *Diacritics* 4, no. 1 (1974), pp. 7–13.

12. I have argued a counterintuitive opposition between dandyism and narcissism in Baudelaire, drawing on Laplanche's analysis of primary masochism in Freud, ibid., pp. 11–13.

13. "A partir du mot *unheimlich* chez Marx," *Critique* 333 (February 1975), pp. 232–253.

14. Benjamin, *Gesammelte Schriften*, vol. 1, p. 612.

15. Ibid., p. 614.

16. Ibid., p. 653.

17. See my comments on Laplanche's analysis of *The Rat Man* (*Le Bulletin de psychologie* 306 [1972–73]), in *Revolution and Repetition* (Berkeley: University of California Press, 1977), p. 100.

18. Benjamin, *Gesammelte Schriften*, vol. 1, p. 646.

19. Ibid., p. 647.

20. Denis Hollier, "Why Are We in America?" *MLN* 93 (December 1978), pp. 990–1006.

21. Michel Leiris, *A Structural Study of Autobiography* (Ithaca, NY: Cornell University Press, 1974).

22. Roberto Calasso, *The Ruin of Kasch*, trans. William Weaver and Stephen Sartarelli (Cambridge, MA: Harvard University Press, 1994), p. 83.

23. Ibid., p. 340.

24. Ibid., p. 28.

25. Maurizio Blondet, *Gli "Adelphi" della dissoluzione: Strategie culturali del potere iniziatico* (Milan: Ares, 1999).

26. Roberto Calasso, *K* (New York: Knopf, 2005), p. 20.

CHAPTER 17

1. Jeffrey Mehlman, "Literature and Collaboration: Benoist-Méchin's Return to Proust," in *Genealogies of the Text: Literature, Psychoanalysis, and Politics in Modern France* (Cambridge: Cambridge University Press, 1995), pp. 53–66.

2. Jeffrey Mehlman, "Flowers of Evil: Paul Morand, the Collaboration, and Literary History," in ibid., pp. 195–216.

Cultural Memory | *in the Present*

Natalie Melas, *All the Difference in the World: Postcoloniality and the Ends of Comparison*

Jonathan Culler, *The Literary in Theory*

Michael G. Levine, *The Belated Witness: Literature, Testimony, and the Question of Holocaust Survival*

Jennifer A. Jordan, *Structures of Memory: Understanding German Change in Berlin and Beyond*

Christoph Menke, *Reflections of Equality*

Marlène Zarader, *The Unthought Debt: Heidegger and the Hebraic Heritage*

Jan Assmann, *Religion and Cultural Memory: Ten Studies*

David Scott and Charles Hirschkind, *Powers of the Secular Modern: Talal Asad and His Interlocutors*

Gyanendra Pandey, *Routine Violence: Nations, Fragments, Histories*

James Siegel, *Naming the Witch*

J. M. Bernstein, *Against Voluptuous Bodies: Late Modernism and the Meaning of Painting*

Theodore W. Jennings, Jr., *Reading Derrida / Thinking Paul: On Justice*

Richard Rorty and Eduardo Mendieta, *Take Care of Freedom and Truth Will Take Care of Itself: Interviews with Richard Rorty*

Jacques Derrida, *Paper Machine*

Renaud Barbaras, *Desire and Distance: Introduction to a Phenomenology of Perception*

Jill Bennett, *Empathic Vision: Affect, Trauma, and Contemporary Art*

Ban Wang, *Illuminations from the Past: Trauma, Memory, and History in Modern China*

James Phillips, *Heidegger's* Volk: *Between National Socialism and Poetry*

Frank Ankersmit, *Sublime Historical Experience*

István Rév, *Retroactive Justice: Prehistory of Post-Communism*

Paola Marrati, *Genesis and Trace: Derrida Reading Husserl and Heidegger*

Krzysztof Ziarek, *The Force of Art*

Marie-José Mondzain, *Image, Icon, Economy: The Byzantine Origins of the Contemporary Imaginary*

Cecilia Sjöholm, *The Antigone Complex: Ethics and the Invention of Feminine Desire*

Jacques Derrida and Elisabeth Roudinesco, *For What Tomorrow . . . : A Dialogue*

Elisabeth Weber, *Questioning Judaism: Interviews by Elisabeth Weber*

Jacques Derrida and Catherine Malabou, *Counterpath: Traveling with Jacques Derrida*

Martin Seel, *Aesthetics of Appearing*

Nanette Salomon, *Shifting Priorities: Gender and Genre in Seventeenth-Century Dutch Painting*

Jacob Taubes, *The Political Theology of Paul*

Jean-Luc Marion, *The Crossing of the Visible*

Eric Michaud, *The Cult of Art in Nazi Germany*

Anne Freadman, *The Machinery of Talk: Charles Peirce and the Sign Hypothesis*

Stanley Cavell, *Emerson's Transcendental Etudes*

Stuart McLean, *The Event and Its Terrors: Ireland, Famine, Modernity*

Beate Rössler, ed., *Privacies: Philosophical Evaluations*

Bernard Faure, *Double Exposure: Cutting Across Buddhist and Western Discourses*

Alessia Ricciardi, *The Ends of Mourning: Psychoanalysis, Literature, Film*

Alain Badiou, *Saint Paul: The Foundation of Universalism*

Gil Anidjar, *The Jew, the Arab: A History of the Enemy*

Jonathan Culler and Kevin Lamb, eds., *Just Being Difficult? Academic Writing in the Public Arena*

Jean-Luc Nancy, *A Finite Thinking*, edited by Simon Sparks

Theodor W. Adorno, *Can One Live after Auschwitz? A Philosophical Reader*, edited by Rolf Tiedemann

Patricia Pisters, *The Matrix of Visual Culture: Working with Deleuze in Film Theory*

Andreas Huyssen, *Present Pasts: Urban Palimpsests and the Politics of Memory*

Talal Asad, *Formations of the Secular: Christianity, Islam, Modernity*

Dorothea von Mücke, *The Rise of the Fantastic Tale*

Marc Redfield, *The Politics of Aesthetics: Nationalism, Gender, Romanticism*

Emmanuel Levinas, *On Escape*

Dan Zahavi, *Husserl's Phenomenology*

Rodolphe Gasché, *The Idea of Form: Rethinking Kant's Aesthetics*

Michael Naas, *Taking on the Tradition: Jacques Derrida and the Legacies of Deconstruction*

Herlinde Pauer-Studer, ed., *Constructions of Practical Reason: Interviews on Moral and Political Philosophy*

Jean-Luc Marion, *Being Given That: Toward a Phenomenology of Givenness*

Theodor W. Adorno and Max Horkheimer, *Dialectic of Enlightenment*

Ian Balfour, *The Rhetoric of Romantic Prophecy*

Martin Stokhof, *World and Life as One: Ethics and Ontology in Wittgenstein's Early Thought*

Gianni Vattimo, *Nietzsche: An Introduction*

Jacques Derrida, *Negotiations: Interventions and Interviews, 1971-1998*, ed. Elizabeth Rottenberg

Brett Levinson, *The Ends of Literature: The Latin American "Boom" in the Neoliberal Marketplace*

Timothy J. Reiss, *Against Autonomy: Cultural Instruments, Mutualities, and the Fictive Imagination*

Hent de Vries and Samuel Weber, eds., *Religion and Media*

Niklas Luhmann, *Theories of Distinction: Re-Describing the Descriptions of Modernity*, ed. and introd. William Rasch

Johannes Fabian, *Anthropology with an Attitude: Critical Essays*

Michel Henry, *I Am the Truth: Toward a Philosophy of Christianity*

Gil Anidjar, *"Our Place in Al-Andalus": Kabbalah, Philosophy, Literature in Arab-Jewish Letters*

Hélène Cixous and Jacques Derrida, *Veils*

F. R. Ankersmit, *Historical Representation*

F. R. Ankersmit, *Political Representation*

Elissa Marder, *Dead Time: Temporal Disorders in the Wake of Modernity (Baudelaire and Flaubert)*

Reinhart Koselleck, *The Practice of Conceptual History: Timing History, Spacing Concepts*

Niklas Luhmann, *The Reality of the Mass Media*

Hubert Damisch, *A Theory of /Cloud/: Toward a History of Painting*

Jean-Luc Nancy, *The Speculative Remark: (One of Hegel's bon mots)*

Jean-François Lyotard, *Soundproof Room: Malraux's Anti-Aesthetics*

Jan Patočka, *Plato and Europe*

Hubert Damisch, *Skyline: The Narcissistic City*

Isabel Hoving, *In Praise of New Travelers: Reading Caribbean Migrant Women Writers*

Richard Rand, ed., *Futures: Of Jacques Derrida*

William Rasch, *Niklas Luhmann's Modernity: The Paradoxes of Differentiation*

Jacques Derrida and Anne Dufourmantelle, *Of Hospitality*

Jean-François Lyotard, *The Confession of Augustine*

Kaja Silverman, *World Spectators*

Samuel Weber, *Institution and Interpretation: Expanded Edition*

Jeffrey S. Librett, *The Rhetoric of Cultural Dialogue: Jews and Germans in the Epoch of Emancipation*

Ulrich Baer, *Remnants of Song: Trauma and the Experience of Modernity in Charles Baudelaire and Paul Celan*

Samuel C. Wheeler III, *Deconstruction as Analytic Philosophy*

David S. Ferris, *Silent Urns: Romanticism, Hellenism, Modernity*

Rodolphe Gasché, *Of Minimal Things: Studies on the Notion of Relation*

Sarah Winter, *Freud and the Institution of Psychoanalytic Knowledge*

Samuel Weber, *The Legend of Freud: Expanded Edition*

Aris Fioretos, ed., *The Solid Letter: Readings of Friedrich Hölderlin*

J. Hillis Miller / Manuel Asensi, *Black Holes / J. Hillis Miller; or, Boustrophedonic Reading*

Miryam Sas, *Fault Lines: Cultural Memory and Japanese Surrealism*

Peter Schwenger, *Fantasm and Fiction: On Textual Envisioning*

Didier Maleuvre, *Museum Memories: History, Technology, Art*

Jacques Derrida, *Monolingualism of the Other; or, The Prosthesis of Origin*

Andrew Baruch Wachtel, *Making a Nation, Breaking a Nation: Literature and Cultural Politics in Yugoslavia*

Niklas Luhmann, *Love as Passion: The Codification of Intimacy*

Mieke Bal, ed., *The Practice of Cultural Analysis: Exposing Interdisciplinary Interpretation*

Jacques Derrida and Gianni Vattimo, eds., *Religion*